Luanne
Campbell
Box 357
Bradford
Ontario
775-2158

D0935970

GINGER—SALUTE TO A STAR

GINGER

Salute to a Star

by

DICK RICHARDS

CLIFTON BOOKS

New England House, New England Street, Brighton BN1 4HN

Registered Office:
Clifton House, 83-117 Euston Road, London N.W.1

First published 1969

Copyright © Dick Richards

*All rights reserved. No part of this
publication may be reproduced, stored in
a retrieval system or transmitted in any
form or by any means, electronic,
mechanical, photocopying, recording, or
otherwise, without the prior permission
of Clifton Books*

SBN 901255 07 6

Printed in Great Britain by
Hazell Watson & Viney Ltd., Aylesbury, Bucks

FOREWORD—A GREETING TO GINGER

This book is an affectionate nosegay to Ginger Rogers, a popular star who, for well over three decades, has provided us with so much entertainment and nostalgia.

I never regarded Ginger as a great actress, but she is a great trouper and a splendid cinema personality. In common with many other young men I fell in love with the screen Ginger in the early 1930's; with her roguish smile, her lithe dancing legs, her gaiety and peppy vitality. Of course, I was fickle. I had other 'crushes' as well. But there was always a place for Ginger and there still is.

This is by no means an authorized biography. One would need to know her better and spend a lot of time with her to have the privilege of writing a definitive biography of Ginger. In any case, it is possible that she is planning, in time, to tell the full and complete story of her thoughts and philosophy, her search for happiness and the successes, setbacks, joys and problems of so many years at the centre of the Hollywood scene.

But here I have recalled memories of occasional meetings, I have talked with many people who knew her, I have read about, viewed again and recalled the 70-odd films that she has made. I hope the book will give a nostalgic kick to the many people who were also growing up during her formative years, and will be read with interest by the many young people who have seen and loved her films on television. I have had fun writing it and I hope you'll have fun reading it.

For, above all things, Ginger Rogers has always been a fun person. DICK RICHARDS

ACKNOWLEDGMENTS

In writing and remembering this book I have wittingly—and unwittingly—been helped considerably by people, books, newspapers and magazines and I gratefully acknowledge that help. I hope I have not omitted anyone who has helped, in however small a way.

The people include Harold Fielding, his press representative Roger Clifford, Ben Lyon, Virginia Mason, Roy Plomley, Edward Everett Horton, Tedwell Chapman, *Photoplay* editor Ken Ferguson, Thornton Freeland, Hobe Morrison of *Variety*, Paul Myers, New York Library Theatre Curator, the staff of the British Film Institute Research Department, Barry Kent, Margaret Courtenay and, of course, Ginger Rogers and her husband William Marshall, whose visit to Britain gave us the idea.

The books include *Steps in Time* by Fred Astaire (Heinemann); *Don't Call Me Madam* by Ethel Merman (W. H. Allen); *Gershwin* by Robert Payne (Robert Hale); *I Blow My Own Horn* by Jesse Lasky (Gollancz); *The Musical Film* by Douglas McVay (Zwemmer/Barnes); *Pictorial History Of The Talkies* by David Blum (Spring Books); *Webster's Unafraid Dictionary* by Leonard Louis Levinson (Collier Books); *Review of Reviews; Movies On TV* by Steven H. Scheuer (Corgi Books); *The Crazy Mirror* by Raymond Durgnat (Faber & Faber).

Newspapers and magazines whose critics, feature writers and reporters I have quoted include: *The Times, Daily Telegraph, Daily Express, Daily Mail, Daily Herald, Sun, Daily Mirror, Daily Sketch, Evening News, Evening Standard, Star, People, Financial Times, Guardian, News Chronicle, Sunday Times, Sunday Express, Observer, Sunday Telegraph, New York Times, New York Herald-Tribune, New York Morning Telegraph, New York Evening Post, National Board of Review Magazine, Time, Spectator, Variety, Photoplay, Picturegoer, Woman, New York Gallery of Modern Art Booklet.*

The publicity staffs of Universal Pictures, Metro-Goldwyn-Mayer Pictures and Columbia Films have been most helpful.

The few lines of 'Night And Day' quoted on page 69 are the copyright of Chappell & Co.; the brief parody of 'Cheek To Cheek' on page 78 is quoted from Fred Astaire's *Steps In Time*.

Acknowledgements are due to RKO, Paramount Pictures, Metro-Goldwyn-Mayer Pictures and the Twentieth Century-Fox Film Co. for permission to reproduce stills from Ginger Rogers' films.

CONTENTS

ILLUSTRATIONS

Chapter 1

STAR SHINES OVER WATERLOO

Ginger Rogers has been an international personality for three decades and, as impresario Harold Fielding has said: 'Out of every 100 people it's certain that at least 95 have heard of her.' To a whole generation of filmgoers she has been part of an irresistible dancing legend with Fred Astaire, helping to spread glamour, fun and nostalgia to millions who have either been ardent fans through the years or at least have enjoyed high spots in her long film career.

The news that she had been booked to appear in a lavish musical show at the Theatre Royal, Drury Lane, stirred many a pulse among everyday, entertainment-loving people.

Waterloo Station in London, like most big-city termini, is glumly functional. It broods over a grey, dispiriting strip of London and methodically concentrates on its heavy task of ferrying hordes of jaded, disillusioned and often irritably tired Londoners from A to Z. There are occasional justifiable bleats from these disgruntled commuters; yet, on the whole, Waterloo fulfils its complicated job with a plodding efficiency.

Unlike some large stations, too depressingly awful even to contemplate without a sharp rise in blood pressure, the station even manages to wear a spurious air of being 'with it'. Perhaps that is a rash overstatement, but at least it boasts some amenities in the shape of a cinema, bookstalls, cigarette, fruit and confectionery kiosks, bars and even the opportunity to go mad and weigh oneself. If you 'collect' stations, then Waterloo isn't a bad example.

But nobody in his right mind would ever regard it as an ideal place for a fiesta. Since the authorities either cannot or will not bring a spot of gaiety even to such ideal sites as Trafalgar, Sloane and Leicester Squares, it is hardly to be expected that Waterloo Station will be given a touch of glamour.

Yet, for a moment on Friday, December 20th 1968, Waterloo Station glowed and had itself a little ball. For a while it was a bridge between London and a Hollywood which was for years a place of fantasy for every cinemagoer but now no longer, alas, exists. It was a brief gay echo of a Hollywood whose stardust has been swamped by smog; a place that has been taken over by Big Business, computers and faceless men in grey flannel suits to whom showmanship is an unknown word and a film is simply an entry on a balance sheet. The overwhelming power of agents, the death of the star system, the taking over of studios by powerful industrial concerns, and the jet-age which has made it easier and more pleasant for many stars to live in Europe or in and around Manhattan, have all helped to turn the busy, hard working, but fun city of Hollywood into a factory largely devoted to churning out television series. I made my first visit to Hollywood in 1947 and my last a couple of years ago. The differences were obvious and sad.

Yet for a fleeting hour Hollywood seemed to come to life in London on that December day with the arrival of Ginger Rogers, whose name has for over 30 years been linked with Hollywood during its most fruitful era. Ginger was not in London on film business. Her mission was the stage which, during her long career, she has tended to neglect because of the demands of the film studios.

It had all begun when Harold Fielding and Bernard Delfont decided that the Broadway musical, *Mame*, was the next attraction needed for Drury Lane Theatre. Even with the exuberant

Harry Secombe as star, its British predecessor, *The Four Musketeers*, had had a shaky run. Frequently it had played to only half-filled houses, to audiences which would have been reasonable in many a smaller theatre but were just not large enough for that expensive showplace, Drury Lane.

What was needed was a big, walloping New York success, with a glittering star and pre-packed publicity, and then Fielding and Delfont suspected that they would be home and dry. *Mame*, with Angela Lansbury, was already a solid Broadway success and was bound to run for a long time. Even when Angela Lansbury left the show to go into *Dear World*, and was replaced by other stars for limited seasons, *Mame* continued its merry success, and as far back as June 1969 had chalked up over 1,300 performances.

Harold Fielding and Bernard Delfont had a hunch that *Mame* was the show for Drury Lane. But what about the star? The two men sat down and listed their choices in order of preference. 'Ginger Rogers' name headed both our lists, quite independently,' says Fielding, and from that moment the wheels started turning.

Getting Ginger for the role of *Mame* was no pushover and Delfont and Fielding realized that negotiations could be long and tricky. Bernard Delfont, a one-time hoofer around variety theatres, is a seasoned impresario who knows all the angles when it comes to pushing a deal. He also has the great advantage over many impresarios of possessing a warm love of the live theatre which amounts almost to an obsession. He prefers his shows to make a profit, but if he thinks a production has merit and yet loses money, he never hollers 'Murder'. He has frequently told me: 'If you get 50 per cent winners then you are batting nicely.'

Harold Fielding, once a velvet-suited child prodigy on the violin, is a small, approachable, alertly energetic man with an affable courtesy. I said that he was small; physically, this is true. But there is nothing small about his thinking and planning when it comes to show business. At first sight there may seem little of the traditional theatrical tycoon about him, but he can be toughly shrewd when it comes to negotiating a deal, and he usually keeps a trump card up his sleeve as a possible clincher.

Delfont and Fielding, partners in this upcoming production, talked over every angle for many months. They knew that a star was essential and that she would not be cheap; that the show itself would be expensive to stage; that it was a gamble which if it didn't come off could leave them sadly in the red.

Still they elected to go on; they did not swerve from their belief that Ginger Rogers could be the star who would bring the necessary aura to the Lane. That aura was what they set out to buy.

The negotiations with Ginger must have been fascinating. After so many years in the cut-and-thrust of the cinema jungle, where money is not only something to spend lavishly and invest carefully but is also a star status symbol, Miss Rogers well knows her worth. She should do. She is one of Hollywood's richest actresses and most provident business women. She is not greedy about money, but she believes that you can't have too much of it if you use it wisely, and she certainly is a staunch advocate of the labourer being worthy of her hire.

Two facts undoubtedly helped the discussions to run smoothly. First, Fielding and Delfont made no secret of the fact that they wanted Ginger for their show very much. They wanted the star magic which, allied to an audience nostalgia, would switch on all the warmth and excitement that a show-place like Drury Lane needs. The desire to see her in person would be irresistible.

On the other hand, Ginger equally made no secret of the fact that she was anxious to appear in London, as something new and exciting in her career. It had to be the right part though. Curiously, she did not think that the combination of herself, *Hello, Dolly!* and London would jell, though she liked the role and clicked with it both on Broadway and on tour.

So when she was invited to take over the part at Drury Lane she thumbed down the proposition, and the role was played by Dora Bryan.

But she had a 'feeling' about *Mame*.

The partners made many transatlantic phone calls at £1 a minute and also many trips to New York and the Coast to discuss the project. By the swimming pool at Ginger's attractive white house overlooking the film country they amicably discussed the problems. A major snag was that the star, who is a great home body, did not really want to uproot for an entire year. Fielding persuaded her reasonably that any shorter contract would not give him and Bernie Delfont a chance of profiting on what would clearly be a remarkably expensive show.

Perhaps Harold Fielding mentioned some of the lush trimmings that they were prepared to provide to make Ginger feel on top of the world? Perhaps it was a minor psychological touch that turned the scale? He scoured London for books, old playbills, old programmes and other paraphernalia connected with the famous Drury Lane Theatre. Any star with greasepaint so firmly under her skin would find it difficult to resist the majesty and atmosphere of the Theatre Royal. And to know that she could reign there for at least a year. . . .

In the end Ginger signed up for 54 weeks, with an option, on a contract worth £250,000. Arguably, this is the largest salary ever paid to an actress playing in the West End.

With a quarter-of-a-million-pound contract tucked away in her safe it is small wonder that when she arrived at Waterloo Station she was looking as radiant as a freshly lit Christmas tree.

Fielding and Delfont were aware from the outset that this production was going to be no pauper's outing. They decided to pull out all the stops and give their Golden Girl the real star treatment.

GINGER—Salute to a Star

The ballyhoo had started when the *Bremen* docked at 1.30 p.m.—90 minutes late because of gales. It was fitting that Ginger and her husband, writer-producer Bill Marshall, should arrive by sea. It was a reminder of the days when stars invariably travelled by liner, when life was more leisurely, more lavish, more ritzy, and it was not necessary for stars to rush madly from country to country, film studio to film studio, huddle in airport V.I.P. lounges, and often arrive tired, crumpled and vexed.

Anyway, with Ginger's Everest of luggage she and her husband didn't have much option but to travel by ship. She brought 118 pieces of luggage, a mass of summer and winter clothes, painting equipment, golf clubs and tennis gear, plus many of those sentimental household trinkets that most women tend to lug around if ever they leave home for more than a couple of weeks.

'I believe in dressing for the occasion,' Ginger has said, 'There's a time for sweater, sneakers and levis and a time for the full-dress jazz. As for the little touches from home, well, a year is quite a long time and they make one *feel* at home.'

How much this mountain of luggage weighed I would not know, but the lady certainly did not travel light and her gear was insured, I gather, for the not inconsiderable sum of £62,000.

Fielding and Delfont had made a calculated risk in planning to do *Mame* with an expensive star, so they cheerfully decided to invest another couple of thousand pounds or so in a giant greeting to Ginger.

The banging of the big drum for their valuable star asset had begun earlier in the day at Waterloo. With a showman's splash Fielding had hired a train, dubbed it 'The Ginger Rogers Mame Express' and let it loose down to Southampton to meet the incoming ship. The Mame Express was loaded with breakfasting, tippling and gossiping newspaper scribes, cameramen, TV and radio gabbers and publicity men. The showing of one of Ginger's best known films, *Top Hat*, put the party in lively spirits.

Nevertheless, Fielding was taking a big chance, and he must have known it. This was the kind of story that was ready-made for any snide reporter in the mood to take the 'mickey'. To many of these young men and women any performer well known and established before they were even born is a fair target. Any performer who was a world favourite long before the Beatles hit the limelight and is still a star is regarded suspiciously; by now he or she ought to be a has-been, they think. Ginger Rogers is in her late fifties, and it is incredible to these young sprigs that she and others of that age are not only still entertaining audiences but doing it with a sparkle and knowhow that show up the careless deficiencies of some of our young actors and actresses.

Ginger makes no secret of her age—though, as I shall show later, she resents the obsessive way in which some people try to make a Federal case out of it, probing and needling. But the indestructible Ginger has campaigned successfully through too many press receptions and interviews to be thrown easily. She coped with gags about her age with brisk good humour.

Perhaps the whole scene was too tempting a target for some of the reporters? To those who never knew it, it is perhaps hard to realize that the glamour, showmanship, spurious glitter and fun of Hollywood in its heyday had a superficial excitement and enchantment that perfectly matched the atmosphere of an extravagant dream factory devoted to providing entertainment for millions. Many who covered the arrival of Ginger Rogers saw it merely as a parody of an old Hollywood legend that they could not really believe happened, not as well-staged fun such as we can well do with in this not-so-merrie olde England.

But Fielding had his reward. In the evening papers and those next morning, the coverage, in words and pictures, was spacious. The stories were mostly lighthearted and tongue-in-the-cheek with a smattering of smart-alec cracks, some witty, some ponderous. But only one was needlessly offensive. Well, I suppose it gave the writer and some of his readers a kick.

For it had to be faced that there was a minute number of people in Britain just raring to crack at the arrival of such American stars as Ginger, Betty Grable and Veronica Lake. For some reason they resented them and bitchily wrote off such visitors as washed up. Out of ignorance or sheer gall they implied that they were living on past reputations, despite the successes they still enjoy in the States.

One man in a letter to a newspaper had the nerve to use the word 'flop' in connection with Ginger. She hadn't even started to rehearse, let alone play the role! But when a star has had the stamina and talent to keep in the front rank for as many years as Ginger Rogers she can take this sort of criticism in her stride.

The 55-piece band of the 1st Battalion of the Worcester Regiment was busily pumping out selections from *Mame*, patiently awaiting the arrival of the ship. Television and newspaper cameras were at the alert. Dockers and rubbernecks waited for the big moment. Still the military band churned out the title song for the umpteenth time. Buffeted by the gales the *Bremen* at last arrived, steaming into dock as proudly as any liner should.

Then at last Ginger appeared on the gangway. She was wearing thigh-length boots and a beige-coloured coat with a huge Russian lynx fur hood that framed her glowing face like an aureole. And what a smile she wore! She advanced a few yards down the gangway while her fellow passengers on the ship cheered and thrust forward for a farewell view.

She stood waving. It was a perfect film star entrance, and the crowd on the dockside rose to it as the band played louder and with more animation after its long wait.

'Welcome, Ginger!' . . . 'Good old Ginger!' then a burst of welcoming cheering. Strangers linked arms and danced to 'Knees up Mother Brown'. *This* was the razzamatazz; *this* was the kind of scene that, on their honeymoon, caused Mary Pickford and Douglas Fairbanks Senior to escape from the crowds surrounding their London hotel by clambering across the roof. This was the sort of Hollywood showmanship that rocked the Savoy when Tom Mix, the cowboy star, once rode his horse into the ballroom.

Much of this type of glamorous, carnival showmanship has disappeared, and who's to say whether or not it is a pity? But as she walked confidently and happily down the gangway it took many people back to nostalgic evenings when they sat with their girl friends in the back rows of cinemas holding hands and avidly watching Norma Shearer, Clark Gable, Spencer Tracy, Katharine Hepburn, Jimmy Cagney, Joan Crawford, Paul Muni, Garbo, Ronald Colman and a host of other spinners of make-believe such as Ginger.

Forgive me if I include myself among the nostalgic. . . .

Camera bulbs popped like fireworks as the Rogers entourage moved to 'The Mame Express'. Its lounge was sumptuously crammed with flowers, interviewers firing questions in between eating lunch and huge dollops of chocolate ice-cream, which Ginger scoffs as passionately as some people dive into peanuts and crisps.

She answered the sensible questions frankly and parried others as adroitly as a tightrope walker, conscious that she would have to answer them all again repeatedly, just as she has had to answer the same old clichés constantly throughout her career. But her friendly smile never wavered.

Waterloo Station again. A fanfare of trumpets from eight of the musicians of the Kneller Hall Military School of Music. She was met by Station Master Don Southorn, with the same courteous ceremony that he produces urbanely for such V.I.P.s as royalty, visiting dignitaries and the major grade of politician. It was quite a long time, though, since a star of even Ginger's reputation had earned the 'Big Hello'.

Welcoming crowds pushed forward to greet the celluloid

favourite; the women shouting 'We love you, Ginger' and the men cheerfully bellowing 'Show us your legs, ducks'. She was half-escorted, half-pushed towards a waiting horse-drawn open landau.

Over the bridge, and the sun began to gleam on the slow-moving Thames—*NOT*, as one columnist good humouredly pointed out, arranged by Harold Fielding! The landau drew up at the Savoy Hotel and Ginger, Bill Marshall and their party moved through the swing doors and were swallowed up.

It was all glorious nonsense; but it was show business, and it had been quite a day. . . .

Chapter 2

SHE CHARLESTONED TO BROADWAY

In many ways Ginger has been lucky. All her life she has had a capacity for hard work, and whether she is working, playing or relaxing sixty seconds spells a minute. Added to talent these are tremendous assets. She also moved into the profession in which she was to become a name—if not one of the screen immortals like Garbo, Gary Cooper, the Gish Sisters, Bogart, Chaplin, Mary Pickford, Marilyn Monroe and a few others—when she was quite a kid.

Yet she has never been what is called a 'child star'; nor did her success come overnight. With a professional instinct blended with a fine screen personality she has worked and battled right from the start for her success.

That is one way in which she was fortunate. The curious and often cruel show-business road has been littered with the shattered neuroses of the moppets who had everything pulling for them from the start. Youngsters like Judy Garland, Mickey Rooney, Liz Taylor, Freddie Bartholomew, Margaret O'Brien and many others all made the grade—and made it big—but at what a cost to nerves, happiness and lost childhood.

It didn't happen like that for Ginger. It was having a go, as well as a natural talent and hard graft, that gave her her early chances.

I am sorry for some of the pampered starlets of today. I have seen them flip their hips across a television screen, bedazzle some producer or casting agent with a roving eye and, presto!

they are pitchforked into a top role in a lavish feature film. Well equipped in many ways they may be; but not necessarily for Instant Stardom.

I have seen debs and typists, models, manicurists and maids flung pell-mell into the cinema élite simply by being at the right place—Chasen's, The White Elephant, the Arethusa, any of the Hiltons, or even at a café in Rome's Via Veneto—at the right time. In walks an impressionable young film-maker with power and a 'star' is born.

Within a month, I've often seen the poison work. I have seen them fly into temperaments of shattering, monumental proportions simply because their dressing room is too poky and small. Or their billing. They have wished damnation on their agents, insulted the columnists and sneered at established performers, before they could even enter a restaurant with grace and presence; and certainly before they could deliver a line with meaning or walk on to a stage or set with confidence. This applies nearly as often, of course, to would-be young Cary Grants and Steve McQueens.

When Ginger and most of her contemporaries who have lasted—people like Rosalind Russell, Bette Davis, Barbara Stanwyck, Joan Crawford—broke into movies no worth-while studio or producer would tolerate such high-handed nonsense. Most of the aspirants were too delighted to get a break to risk putting on the uppity. They were glad enough to work. Sometimes it was stormy weather but if the girl had what it took she rode the storm.

Those proverbial butterflies were doing their proverbial, nervy fandango in the pit of the stomach of a lissom, eager redhead; why a fragile, dainty creature like a butterfly should cause internal tremors has always puzzled me, but Miss Ginger Rogers' torso was fluttering.

And why not? It was her first big chance on Broadway, she wasn't yet 19 and it was Christmas Day 1929.

She Charlestoned to Broadway

Top Speed, a musical comedy which made little impact on American theatrical history, ran at the 46th Street Theatre for 102 performances and then folded, having completed its job of entertaining indulgent audiences for a few months. It was a lightweight romantic comedy about two poor but honest American stockbrokers who gatecrashed a smart Canadian hotel and 'romanced' a millionaire's daughter.

But for Ginger it was the beginning. Charlie Morrison, boss of the Hollywood Mocambo Club, had seen her in vaudeville and mentioned her name to Bert Kalmar and Harry Ruby, who were looking for a lively soubrette for their new musical comedy.

Ginger was signed as the second girl lead in *Top Speed*, and had only one real chance to stand out. That was singing a song called 'Hot and Bothered'. It brought her her first notices from major newspapers. The performance of this lively little redhead impressed two newspapermen of surprisingly different stature.

Drama critic Brooks Atkinson came right out and wrote: 'She is an impudent young thing who carries youth and humour to a point where they are completely charming.' Walter Winchell, not, I trust, prodded by one of his leg-men, also found Ginger 'completely charming'.

In the chorus was a man named Hermes Pan, later to influence the Rogers career considerably as the dance director of so many of the Astaire-Rogers pictures. More important, in the audience was a film man named Walter Wanger. Something clicked in his brain. He saw the girl's happy effervescence and the oomph which she projected and which landed right in the laps of the audience. Wanger saw a potential star. He wasn't wrong and he waved a contract in front of her.

In a minor way, Ginger Rogers had started to make it on a slippery ladder. Not all have climbed it, but for her it has led to stardom, world renown, riches, five marriages, but now, I believe, an inner contentment.

It turned out to be a bumper Christmas present but amid all the backstage frenzy of a first night it is unlikely that Ginger had time to remember then how it had all begun.

A lot of people think that Ginger Rogers is a Texas girl. That's not so. She was born Virginia Katharine McMath on a July day in 1911 in Independence, Missouri. Later, President Harry Truman, also born in Independence, was to gag to Ginger: 'So you've come home to steal my thunder, eh?'

Ginger's childhood, though she claims that it was full of love, certainly sounds as if it was unsettled—perhaps no disadvantage for someone who was very early to be plunged into the showbiz millstream. But to be kidnapped twice can be a traumatic experience for a child.

Her father was an electrical engineer and it is rumoured that his parents were an acute problem to him, as they strove to control his life even to early manhood. They had met in a Kansas City dance-hall. A pick-up? Could be, but it has happened to many young couples who have enjoyed happy married laughs and lives. But his parents had a fixation that their son had married beneath him when he wed Lela.

When Ginger's parents were estranged she was twice kidnapped and on each occasion the cause was mischief-making by her father's parents. No harm came to Ginger, but it could not have been much emotional fun to find herself as bait in a perpetual tug-o'-war.

Eventually it worked out. She was given over legally to her mother's care and she was only 11 when her father died. Her mother remarried, her second husband being an insurance man named John Rogers. ('A darling!' says Ginger.) Though the marriage sundered a few years later Ginger has nothing but tender memories of him.

But it is obvious why she is so closely attached to her mother, still a strong, spry character. Ginger was the second of her mother's three children. The first died in infancy; the third was stillborn. Inevitably, Ginger and her mother were drawn together.

A book could be written about 'showbiz mums'—funny, sad, satirical. I could contribute a few edgy paragraphs. There was the time, for instance, when I swotted up the history of the Tower of London to act as a guide to young Margaret O'Brien, for to see the Tower was her greatest desire. The day before the rendezvous Margaret's mum decided to light out to Rome to meet a friend. Does anybody need a few frayed memories of the Tower? And I wonder if Margaret remembers, or if her mother ever realized the disappointment she gave to her now grown-up child?

The book could be illuminating.

When a youngster starts in films she obviously must have someone around whom she trusts and who can look after her creature comforts. But many of the mums hang on for the trips and the red-carpet treatment that their talented offspring provide.

The time comes when showbiz mums should be shed. Some of them start to irk producers with their smiling, ever-increasing, impossible demands for their little ones. Long after the little moppet has nibbled and gnawed fractiously through the umbilical cord mum is still around, still demanding, the smile less attractive, more desperate.

Could Lela Rogers be brought into such a book? Possibly. But, on the evidence, I would think it would be unfair. She has been a hard worker all her life in the very jungle in which her daughter has been launched. She must know many of the answers. And, I believe, protected her daughter from many snags.

Ginger has been quoted as saying: 'The first film I made was *Kitty Foyle*. My mother made all those with Fred Astaire.' Possibly she did say it gaggingly, but I would put it down as a quip turned out by one of those early would-be Neil Simons employed by the studios to produce 'Remarks To Suit Any Occasion' for their stars.

I met Lela Rogers only once. That was very briefly in the foyer of London's staid Brown's Hotel. The astonishment of Forrest Tucker and Dane Clark, who stayed there when I recommended Brown's to them as a substitute for the 'regular circuit', where they could find no peace and their bills were monumental, was equalled only by the astonishment of the hotel when they realized that tough guys on films are usually the mildest, most tractable, characters off duty.

Mrs. Rogers, making her first visit to Europe, was in London to see her daughter open in *Mame*. Something went wrong with communications, so I never got the interview I wanted. All Lela said was: 'It's all wunnerful, and Ginger will be wunnerful, too.' It was not exactly helpful, but there was no doubt about a mother's pride.

Lela Rogers has contributed much to Ginger's success. There are some stage mothers who sit around their daughters' dressing rooms like vultures. They seem to think one is not visiting to get a story but to sink one's fangs into their daughters' swan-like necks like a touring Dracula. Others insist on answering all the questions poised at their star daughters. Others, again, just sit around, not even, apparently, enjoying the ride, and one wonders 'Why?'

Some, however—and Lela Rogers is one—work shrewdly to further their daughters' careers. As a result, Lela Rogers has had many skirmishes with Hollywood tycoons and has probably frequently got into their hair. But Ginger, it would seem, has rarely lost out.

As Ginger has said: 'Even when one is of an age to make one's own decisions there are many times when it is great to be able to go back and talk it over with the people one loves—one's family.'

All her life Lela Rogers has been a fighter and battler and much of it has brushed off on Ginger in that, like her mother, she has never flinched from any problem. Lela has been caught up in national politics and the equally tricky problem of studio politics; always she has fought for what she thought was right.

Lela Rogers started Ginger off quite casually when her daughter was only five. She managed to get her hired to appear in some nondescript advertising films which were being made in Kansas City, where they were then living. Lela even directed some of them, though her experience as a director was not exactly vast.

These films were Ginger's introduction to the heady atmosphere of film studios. Even then she probably picked up unconsciously a feeling for the discipline and bustle of a studio which would stand her in good stead when she was launched eventually into a 'real' one. Yet to Ginger it was all some kind of happy game.

Then Ginger 'lost' her mother for a while. The energetic, ubiquitous Mrs. Rogers went west to try her luck in Hollywood. There, under the name of Lela Leibrand, she pumped out scripts for such stars of the silent days as Theda Bara, with a heart-fluttering quiver on every page.

Some of them were for a child star named Baby Marie Osborne, who, in those far-off days, was something akin to the later Shirley Temple. It is ironic that later, her fame having briefly waxed and waned, Baby Marie was to become Ginger's film stand-in. The film business can be a strange, scary affair of scenic railway ups and downs.

As soon as Lela was settled in she sent for her daughter. Young Ginger was only six but she could almost instantly have joined the child star brigade. Lela by now knew a lot of people and the cute child was spotted by several Big Noises in Hollywood. They all made appropriate sub-noises which added up to suggestions that she should be in their films.

It must have been a temptation, but Lela resolutely resisted it. She considered Ginger too young to be subjected to all the possible headaches and heartaches that could crop up as a child actress, and to my mind this decision proves Mrs. Rogers to have been a wise, understanding woman.

25

Then came World War I, and Ginger was sent back to her grandparents in Kansas City. Lela went to Washington to work on a Marine Corps magazine until the Armistice, when she rejoined her daughter in Kansas City. It was there that the seeds of Ginger's future career were sown, yet even then it was all casual and unpremeditated. After the war Mrs. Rogers got herself a job as a reporter on the *Kansas City Post*, and later moved to the *Fort Worth Record*, where she became society and drama correspondent. Environment started to work for Ginger. Their little home became a rendezvous for local theatrical folk and those passing through.

In a booklet about her daughter's career Mrs. Rogers has written: 'Ginger Rogers was the most beautiful baby anyone could have wished for, and began dancing before she could even walk. At the age of three she was singing the popular numbers of the day, the words pronounced in her own baby way, but right on the nose with the time and the beat. Actors, musicians and opera singers were guests in my house for after-theatre snacks of southern fried chicken, biscuits and honey. By the age of fifteen Ginger had met them all, plus the local theatre managers, who were my friends.'

Ginger and her stepfather, John Rogers, used to put on fun shows in the parlour to entertain the guests. They were probably not so hot, just impromptu whoopees, but the guests Chez Rogers seemed to lap them up. They all agreed that this young, animated child was a natural for the stage. 'You'll never be able to keep her out of the theatre,' said one happy gentleman, solemnly waving a leg of southern fried.

Mrs. Rogers was flattered, but not convinced. In Hollywood, and even in the comparatively small towns of Kansas City and Fort Worth, she had seen enough of show business to know that it could be cruelly harsh. To be sure of making the grade was almost as impossible as to be certain of winning the pools.

'She's going to college first,' she said flatly. 'Then, if she wants the stage, she can have it.'

She Charlestoned to Broadway

Fair enough, but Ginger never did make college. The stage won right from the outset.

It was the time when all the local kids were dance-crazy and Ginger was among them. She had a particular excitement for that peppy, cockeyed, leggy dance, the Charleston, even though she admits to being a plump teenager. She picked up her first tuition in the dance which was to set her twinkling feet towards the stars from an old-time retired pro named 'Daddy' Wilson, who lived near by. 'Daddy' was now a bit rheumaticky, grey-haired and rheumy-eyed, but when it came to the Charleston he could still shake an agile leg. Ginger would go to his house and he would put her through her paces till the rhythm and the beat of the dance became second nature to her. She was ready when the chance came.

There was a big touring band run by a man named Henry Santrey and when he was playing locally he hit on the idea of promoting the band by cashing in on the new craze. He would run a gala Charleston contest.

He talked it over with Lela Rogers and Bob O'Donnell, the up-and-coming manager of the Interstate Theatre Circuit. They agreed that the contest could be a great promotion. As soon as it was announced a couple of dozen local youngsters entered their names. But not Ginger Rogers. Lela put her foot down and forbade it.

'Supposing you won?' she explained patiently to her disappointed daughter. 'Remember, I've been in on this contest from the beginning. Can't you imagine the howl? Everybody would think the whole thing had been rigged to get publicity in my paper.'

These days a youngster of Ginger's age would have cried blue murder at not getting her way. Instead she had a quiet word with Bill Hart, who managed the Majestic Theatre where the Charleston Carnival was due to break loose, and also with Bob O'Donnell. They were both on Ginger's side but could see that her mother had a valid point. Bill O'Donnell made one final plea. 'There isn't a single entry in the column who can hold a candle to Ginger in the Charleston. It will *make* the show with her in it.' Lela remained adamant.

Then, suddenly, she was phoned by O'Donnell: 'Lela, come over to the theatre. It's urgent.' She went and there was young Ginger dancing a blue streak in front of the band as it whipped into a frenzied Charleston. Her feet seemed not to touch the ground. Her face was alight. The whole scene radiated some crazy kind of ecstasy.

The music stopped; Lela Rogers looked at her daughter and she knew what had to happen.

She sat up all night to make a dress for Ginger. 'It was all silvery,' remembers Ginger, 'a kind of white crêpe romaine. I don't think they even make the material any more.' Though some of the competitors were dancing in pairs, Ginger elected to go solo, won the local heat and qualified for the finals.

This was showbiz-de-luxe, for the finals were being held on the swanky roof room of the Baker Hotel in Dallas, some 25 miles away. The journey did not worry Ginger—hadn't she already travelled to Hollywood?—but the event did. Possibly she sensed deep down that this could be the beginning of something big.

Rigged out in another new dress, black this time and more suited for a girl of 20 than a 14-year-old, Ginger plunged once more into the contest. The heady tournament went on for a couple of hours, which is a great deal of Charleston, and soon the competitors, who were picked by audience applause, were whittled down to two. Ginger and a lad named Billy Daniels.

Normally a pretty lass like Ginger would have had most of the audience behind her, especially when opposed to a boy. But there was a chauvinistic snag. This was Dallas, and Billy Daniels came from Dallas. Ginger was from Fort Worth, and the two Texas towns were cut-throat rivals which claimed that each was bigger, better and brighter than the other—even arguing as to which shoeshine boys could work up the slicker polish. Young Ginger was operating in hostile territory.

But the audience played it fair. Twice the two tied in volume of applause, and a third 'play-off' was needed. Maybe the audience's heart went out to a stripling who showed the talent, stamina and guts to keep on an even keel with an elder boy in such a taxing marathon as the Charleston. On the third call there was no question which was the winner.

Ginger was given a gold medal which eventually was inscribed: 'Ginger Rogers, Charleston Champion of Texas.' I have a feeling that even the Oscar she was to win some 15 years later did not give her a bigger thrill than that medal, which was to be a passport to stardom.

From that moment life became a whirl for young Ginger and she was lucky to have a mother able to act as a buffer, negotiator, chaperone and general adviser. She never saw school or real home life again until she had become a topliner. Life for Ginger became a montage of stuffy trains, clattering wheels, poky dressing rooms, snatched meals at stations, rehearsals, band calls, changes of costume, tiny hotels, new people, different theatres, different audiences, early train calls, packing. It may not have been the most refined University but, by heaven, she learned about show business and life.

The Charleston contest started her career in the toughest way, on tour. The prize, apart from the medal, was a contract to play the Interstate Circuit for several months at $300 a week, which meant a lot of money for Ginger, but also a lot of work.

'My mother decided that my solo Charleston act needed pepping up for the tough theatres ahead. She remembered that in the finals at the Dallas hotel there had been a couple of runners-up from Houston. One was a strapping 17-year-old boy named Earl Leach and his partner was a peppy girl named Josephine Butler. The fact that they both had red hair gave mother an idea.'

GINGER—Salute to a Star

Lela wired them, offered them a job with Ginger—and that's how 'Ginger Rogers and the Redheads' came into being. They really had it tough. In those days, when vaudeville in America was big business, five shows a day were common, which meant that a performer could virtually be a prisoner in his poky dressing room from midday till last thing at night, except when released to go on stage. There were one-night stands. There were weeks out, but not too many in the case of Ginger and her partners, for the act was lively, up-to-the-minute and happy. But it was all experience.

The act eventually broke up and Ginger turned to doing a solo act in which she sang and danced. Her first appearance at Memphis was something of a disaster and the manager wanted her out. Somehow she survived the first-show nerves and in the evening show she was her own vivacious, on-the-ball self. She was *not* tossed off the bill.

The next two or three years saw Ginger and her mother touring the vastness of the States, where one good act could last performers for a year if they were prepared to move around the country. Lela Rogers made Ginger's costumes, argued money and billing, warded off stage door johnnies and wrote much of Ginger's material, for which she took 20 per cent of the soubrette's earnings. It was a good team. Without temperament, Ginger would wait in the wings, go on, captivate the audience and then go back to the dressing room until the next show. To her it was a job, and one she enjoyed, for she was doing what came naturally by singing and hoofing.

Ginger had played cafés and joints in Galveston and starred in a road tour which collapsed—not without dignity, but with little acclaim—in St. Louis. Now she was forging ahead as a good solid act in the Midwest and Southern theatres. She had been billed as 'The Original John Held Jr. Girl', a title which at the time probably meant a great deal in prestige, but which now must be a puzzlement to most of us. I can only say that Held Jr., the mystery man, had a transient reputation on the

4# GINGER—Salute to a Star

Lela wired them, offered them a job with Ginger—and that's how 'Ginger Rogers and the Redheads' came into being. They really had it tough. In those days, when vaudeville in America was big business, five shows a day were common, which meant that a performer could virtually be a prisoner in his poky dressing room from midday till last thing at night, except when released to go on stage. There were one-night stands. There were weeks out, but not too many in the case of Ginger and her partners, for the act was lively, up-to-the-minute and happy. But it was all experience.

The act eventually broke up and Ginger turned to doing a solo act in which she sang and danced. Her first appearance at Memphis was something of a disaster and the manager wanted her out. Somehow she survived the first-show nerves and in the evening show she was her own vivacious, on-the-ball self. She was *not* tossed off the bill.

The next two or three years saw Ginger and her mother touring the vastness of the States, where one good act could last performers for a year if they were prepared to move around the country. Lela Rogers made Ginger's costumes, argued money and billing, warded off stage door johnnies and wrote much of Ginger's material, for which she took 20 per cent of the soubrette's earnings. It was a good team. Without temperament, Ginger would wait in the wings, go on, captivate the audience and then go back to the dressing room until the next show. To her it was a job, and one she enjoyed, for she was doing what came naturally by singing and hoofing.

Ginger had played cafés and joints in Galveston and starred in a road tour which collapsed—not without dignity, but with little acclaim—in St. Louis. Now she was forging ahead as a good solid act in the Midwest and Southern theatres. She had been billed as 'The Original John Held Jr. Girl', a title which at the time probably meant a great deal in prestige, but which now must be a puzzlement to most of us. I can only say that Held Jr., the mystery man, had a transient reputation on the

American stage in the twenties, representing a typical college boy, complete with Oxford bags—the ultra-wide trousers which we youngsters flaunted with pride. (I wonder now how we dare criticize the ultra-narrow trousers of modern youngsters?)

But by now Ginger was getting ambitious, and her mother was all for it. There came a time when obviously one had to break out of the provincial 'grind' and look towards New York, where the action was.

She was 17 when she appeared with comedian Willie Howard in an act which, as a speciality, first played for 18 weeks in Chicago, and followed the Windy City engagement by a booking at the Paramount Theatre on Broadway. This booking with the Paramount-Publix circuit really projected Ginger. She sang, she danced and she gave recalations about the anumals, including Mama Nyceroserous and Papa Hippopapumis, in 'baby-talk'. In cold print it all sounds fairly nauseating, but it was different, the audiences liked it, and even to this day Ginger occasionally lapses into baby-talk, though purely as a gag for her chums.

She was also beginning to make fairly good money and was performing in the theatre fringe where big bookers and producers were liable to sit up and take notice of a peppy soubrette who could bring a zing to the musical revuettes in which she was featured. Whether or not Ginger was conscious of this I don't know. She just loved dancing so she would have given everything on stage anyway; though I am sure that the $350 a week (at a time when the dollar really was worth five shillings) was an added incentive.

After these shows on the Paramount-Publix circuit Ginger headlined a show with Eddie Lowry and his band which played St. Louis for 32 weeks and Chicago's Oriental Theatre for another 18. Willie Howard, the comedian, and Paul Ash, who had booked her for the Paramount circuit, both realized that here was a girl who stood out like a mink coat in Macy's department store. Howard taught her the art of 'milking' an audience. It isn't easy. It means sizing up an audience, quickly deciding on its mood—whether it wants comedy, sentiment, dazzling dancing or just 'schmaltz'—and giving it to them quickly. Ginger learned to sock it to 'em from the moment she burst through the wings.

Ash, on the other hand, taught her volumes about timing, a hint of when the audience has had enough of one mood, how long to hold a gag, how long to wait before putting over the next. This knowledge was to become instinctive with Ginger and a sharp asset for her in films.

Much of this experience was fairly tatty, but it had one advantage. It helped to steer an 'amateur' Ginger, who had started out tremulously with Her Redheads, into a budding pro.

It was Charles Morrison, boss of Hollywood's Mocambo Club, who had spotted Ginger's potential, you will remember. It led to her appearance in *Top Speed*, in which she played Babs Green, the second feminine lead, in a cast which included Irene ('Dimples') Delroy, Lester Allen, Paul Frawley and Harland Dixon. You would have to be a very spry student of Broadway's theatrical history to remember these names now, but, however remotely, Ginger had made her first significant step towards the big time. The hard-working grind of five-shows-a-day variety was behind her. She must have felt like the groundboy at a soccer club who is suddenly listed to play for the first team.

As already mentioned, it was with this show that Ginger had her first heady sniff of notices from the big papers. The *New York Sun* benevolently described the show as 'often very funny, thanks to Lester Allen and Ginger Rogers'. Willela Waldorf of the *Evening Post* (and I'd be surprised if Miss Waldorf's name was not a whipped up, phony pen-name dreamed up in her office) was moved to write: 'A young person, identified in the program as Ginger Rogers, manages to be agile, amusing and even distinctive as a singing and dancing comedienne'. I imagine that Miss Waldorf must have been a prime favourite

She Charlestoned to Broadway

in the Rogers dressing room when she read that champagne praise.

But Ginger kept her shrewd head. Though a teenager and already recognized as one of Broadway's up-and-coming talents, she never lived it up. She never has. Her work has always been her chief concern.

Top Speed led to a second, even bigger, Broadway beckoning. She appeared in a show called *Girl Crazy*, which opened at the Alvin Theatre in October 1930. The States was still glowing over the achievements of its current hero, Rear-Admiral Richard Byrd. He was then as much of an idol as America's astronauts today. Maybe more so, for there weren't as many of him. At about the time when Ginger was striving to conquer Broadway, Byrd was on his first chilly expedition to the Antarctic, had made the first flight over the South Pole and discovered the Edsel Ford mountains and Marie Byrd Land.

Yet, amid this Homeric success, America was still badly under the weather, recovering from a late 1929 Wall Street crash which had caused frantic suicides, ruination to many and the macabre spectacle of worthless money being torn up and hurled like ticker-tape from skyscraper windows.

It was during the Depression—a difficult, pessimistic time—that *Girl Crazy* opened, produced by Alex Aarons and the late Vincent Freedley. It ran for only 200 or so performances and I wish I could think it was simply the Depression that caused it to dive after only a few months. But I read the book by Guy Bolton and Jack McGowan recently and shuddered. It was a corny, hill-billy story, set in Custerville, in which some city slickers invaded a dude ranch; it is significant that the show never invaded London.

What kept *Girl Crazy* alive, despite its now bewhiskered gags, was the bright musical score by George Gershwin. Matched to Ira Gershwin's lyrics the show was away to a head start against which the Depression, for a while, never stood a chance.

In a *Woman* magazine series Ginger told Joan Reeder that she was invited to the Gershwins' house one night to listen to some music. 'That's when I first heard the *Girl Crazy* music, but I never even realized that I was being considered for a part, let alone the lead,' Ginger told Miss Reeder.

For Ginger it was an evening to remember. The supremely talented composer, who was to die so tragically early, perhaps not even fulfilling his richest promise, played the songs from *Girl Crazy* with that champagne-and-white-tie touch that distinguished his lighter songs.

That evening Ginger forged a friendship with George and Ira that ended only with George's death at the premature age of 39. She also fell in love with such songs as 'I'm Bidin' My Time', 'But Not For Me' and that wry love song that has become a standard, 'Embraceable You'. Little did she realize that soon she would be singing them nightly at the Alvin. 'But Not For Me' was her favourite. It was a sentimental song that could hardly fail to pluck at the heart of any youngster who had ever been in love—as, briefly, Ginger had been.

But 'Embraceable You' was her big hit in the show. It was also to be the song to which people would respond years after George Gershwin wrote his last love ballad.

Things were shaping up nicely for the girl from Independence. For the first time her name twinkled among the many that shone over Broadway and beckoned to customers like an Armenian carpet-seller to a bizarre market place. She was also being paid the pleasant sum of $1,000 a week, which with other show business engagements was comfortably eased up to $1,500.

But Ginger was to learn swiftly in her career that things do not always turn out as dreamed. The show had originally been planned for Bert Lahr, but he was not available. Still, it was a good cast: Allen Kearns, the De Marcos and an old chum of Ginger's, Willie Howard. Even in the pit orchestra were names that were to spread lustre in the world of show business. Red

She Charlestoned to Broadway

Nichols' orchestra boasted such musicians as Phil Ohman, Gene Krupa, Benny Goodman, Glenn Miller and Jimmy Dorsey—talent enough to keep any cast on its toes.

Ginger was playing Molly, postmistress of Custerville, a rural place on which a Broadway playboy and a bunch of svelte Broadway cuties descended to start a dude ranch. But playing the wife of the man running the local gambling saloon was another girl getting her first chance on the Great White Way (as it used to be known). She was Ethel Merman, a lusty young woman who, like Ginger, had also done her hardworking stint around the vaudeville houses and cafés.

From what one reads, and from what one hears from those around Broadway at the time, Miss Merman took the show in her hands and flung it into the audience's lap, gift-packaged. *Girl Crazy* made two stars. Ethel Merman, undoubtedly. She had three songs which she belted with such a devil-may-care zest that she practically rocketed the first night audience to the chandeliers. They were 'Boy! What Love Has Done For Me', 'Delilah' and 'I Got Rhythm'. With these three songs, adroitly woven for Miss Merman's tonsils, she was accepted at once as an overnight star.

Nobody else in the cast could compete with Ethel Merman's cast-iron lungs. But, in a different way, *Girl Crazy* also made a star of Ginger Rogers.

In her autobiography, *Call Me Madam*, Ethel Merman writes candidly: 'Ginger was pretty, she could act, she could dance, but no one called her The Voice. Ginger's voice was a pleasing one, but small. The way she sang "Embraceable You" was charming, but the songs she sang didn't require power.'

Ginger had no need to worry. Ethel Merman was, without bitchiness, saying the simple truth when she wrote that Ginger's voice was 'small'. But she was pretty, she could act and she could dance. With such equipment she was well able to face the future with confidence.

That future was to be Hollywood.

35

Chapter 3

HOLLYWOOD BECKONS

Ginger Rogers has frequently insisted that she is a person of the theatre. She has been quoted as saying: 'All my breaks came in New York. I am really a Broadway Babe.' In a way, that is perfectly true. Her background was vaudeville. Now that she is less enchanted with the films of today she has turned again to the stage, taken up its nightly challenge, and succeeded both in *Hello, Dolly!* and in *Mame*, as well as in a variety of summer stock shows and tours.

Yet to most minds she is essentially an integral part of the cinema, just as when I was a nipper in short pants the cinema meant to me Tom Mix, Mary Pickford, Hoot Gibson and William S. Hart and, of course, Chaplin. I'm not suggesting that Ginger's a contemporary of these. It's just that all through the years, to me, certain people have been 'theatre', others 'variety', others 'radio' and some rare and beautiful people have meant 'the pictures'. She is one of the milky way of stars who for several years have, through the screen, brought glamour and kicks to our leisure moments. They have helped to keep the cinema attractively magnetic as a major form of popular entertainment. The name of Ginger Rogers is representative of Hollywood, which, in turn, stands for daft old fan magazines, extravagance, intriguing whims, backstage politics, the occasional scandal and a world of fantasy. In many ways it is now different, but somehow the old aura still clings.

Ginger, a frank, honest woman, would not, I fancy, describe

36

herself as one of the great actresses of our generation. No Sarah Bernhardt. She is also conscious that many of her films have been merely routine and, some of them, fairly dreadful. On *Desert Island Discs* on the BBC she was asked by Roy Plomley to admit the films she had made which she particularly disliked. A couple of titles bubbled out. Then she laughed and said 'Let's forget that'—or words to that effect.

But while never deliberately settling for trash, Ginger has always been mainly concerned with appearing in pictures that will give people enjoyment and relaxation, rather than great 'message' epics. Since films and actors in the lighter entertainment bracket rarely get acclaimed or pick up awards (why do people think that it is necessarily easier to play a Walter Matthau or Jack Lemmon comedy role than a solemn, dramatic classical one?), neither Ginger nor her films have ever been scrutinized and analysed like the work of 'weightier' directors and actors. Ginger's contribution to the screen has too often (with the exception, perhaps, of her scintillating song-and-dance saga with Fred Astaire) been simply taken for granted. It is a cross that many 'light' actors have had to learn to bear.

But what Ginger has brought abundantly to the cinema is usually a tonic or a chance to relax for the man or his wife drably nagged by the everyday round of office work, factory chores, household stints and bills, bills and bills. A few shillings is an entrance fee to a never-never haven where people have problems but they are all solved in the end, and where not every man or woman is headed like a space capsule towards a psychiatrist's couch or a mental home. For the man and his wife regulated each morning by the seven o'clock alarm a bit of froth and foolishness on the screen is not a bad palliative.

The qualities that this actress has brought to the screen have stood firm. They are strengths that have seen her through over 30 years in a ruthless atmosphere where you are only as exciting as your last picture. You are allowed two, or at the most three, indifferent films, but after that 'Watch it, sister.

Mind your step, brother'. There is always someone waiting to jostle you from your pinnacle and move in to take over.

If you lead a quiet, reserved life then the local columnists damn you as snooty. If you are an extrovert, as Errol Flynn was, you can run straight into a scandal. Your work not only has to satisfy your boss and his shareholders, but also the often cynical, but ever watchful critics. Above all you have to please the Big Spenders, the public whose bottoms fill cinema seats and whose word of mouth can sometimes make you but equally easily break you. There is nothing quite so vulnerable as a slipping cinema idol.

Ginger's qualities are several. She has an insatiable appetite for work, even though she is sufficiently prosperous not to have to do another stroke for the rest of her life. Repeatedly she has been asked: 'Why do you do it?' She shrugs and smiles: 'There's nothing Freudian about it—or me. I work because it is fun, it is nice to know that you are giving pleasure to people, and anyway I detest idling.'

She's as disciplined as a well-trained shepherd's dog. This intense discipline means tht she takes direction smoothly and keeps to the time- and money-saving habits of being on the set at the right time, knowing her lines and delivering them with the minimum of fuss. Spencer Tracy, one of the great ones, once summed up that those three qualities, plus making sure the money was right and that the script was written so that he had occasional days off for fishing, were his idea of the Acting Method.

Not that Ginger's a Yes Woman. She will fight a producer, director or an equal star with a tangy tenacity if she believes that her suggestion is in the interests of the picture or the show; but her arguments are based on experience and conviction, not just for the sake of blowing a star temperament. She also has a sharp instinct for technique on the screen, based on what she has learned in over 70 forays into the jungle. Add to this a sunny sense of fun and a perky, lively sense of humour on screen which helps occasionally to make an indifferent line seem to crackle with pert wit. But that's acting.

Any one of these qualities is useful for urging an actress to the top. The combination of the lot is as near as is possible an insurance for keeping her there. The combination doesn't necessarily make an actress eligible for a place with the screen immortals. But it makes her a professional to respect, one whom any producer would be glad to hire and any audience delighted to watch.

The small-town redhead was 20 when, with Lela faithfully at the alert, she went to tackle the long Hollywood haul. She may have been young by the standards of those days, but she was no greenhorn. She had come through the toughest show business academy of the time. In towns all over the States, some large, some mere dumps, and in face of all kinds of audience, she had survived. She had lived in modest hotels and cheap, crummy lodgings. She had met the big-timers, those who were slipping like a car going downhill without brakes and those whom the fickle finger of fate had decided early would never make the grade.

She wasn't hard-bitten, tough or disillusioned, but she had learned that it takes all kinds of people and places to give you a show business education. Unlike some, she hadn't been hauled out of a soda fountain or a department store and given the big build-up.

No, she wasn't tough; but she wasn't entirely starry-eyed either. When she reached Hollywood in 1931 she had already been married and divorced, the first of five attempts to find the secret of a happily married life.

Why, she had even made some films.

The first bid of Ginger's nap-hand in the matrimonial stakes happened in 1928, when, during a brief lay-off period at the Chicago Oriental Theatre, she ran into Jack Culpepper, a lad she had known when she was a kid in Texas. They weren't exactly childhood sweethearts but they had been good friends, and Ginger is an outgiving person who gladly welcomes the sight of an old chum.

Jack Culpepper had changed his name to Jack Pepper and was plodding away earning a humble living as a dancer. He was tall, husky, good-looking—the entire package deal for a girl whose emotions had hardly been touched—and they married. Not, it is rumoured, with the maternal blessing of Mrs. Rogers.

There was a brief honeymoon and then the eager young couple started out on the road as a double act called 'Ginger and Pepper'. The name of the act turned out to be hotter than the results. The act folded dismally and so, after ten months, did the marriage. It was to be the first of a number of matrimonial misfires for the girl who has constantly admitted that 'as far as love is concerned' she was a very late grower-up. Meanwhile, though, Ginger was far too busy and caught up in the merry-go-round of show business to worry overmuch about an error which probably did neither of them much harm and maybe brought both a few invaluable months of happiness and experience in weathering the pains of growing up.

You will remember that that shrewd film man, Walter Wanger, was at the first night of her Broadway debut in *Top Speed*. He very rightly saw in her the raw material of someone who had the magic and personality to make a name in films. Wanger took along one of the sage pioneers of the cinema, Jesse Lasky, and she was signed to star in some Paramount films.

They were made in New York, while Ginger was labouring for eight shows a week in *Top Speed*. She would spend the day at the studio, except for matinées, and then leap across to the theatre just in time to make up. It was an appalling day's schedule for a young woman, but Ginger lapped it up, and it is probably the key to her present stamina and ability to work for hours at full stretch.

Hollywood beckons

There was a one-reel short called *Office Blues*, directed by Mort Blumenstock. This is now merely something for the records, but it is interesting because in it Ginger sang a couple of songs called 'Dear Sir' and 'We Can't Get Along'—and there's a tiny bonus for anybody who can now sing either of these songs in full. That bonus goes for the composer too, for I doubt if he will recall the songs. He was a young man hired by Paramount to pound a piano, rehearse with singers and provide very impromptu background music for these films. His name happens to be Johnny Green, and he recently supervised all the music for the Oscar-laden picture, *Oliver!* As far as I'm concerned he is memorable for having written, among many others, such enchanting songs as 'Body and Soul' and 'I Cover The Waterfront'.

Among Ginger's other chores was to sing a couple of ditties in a picture called *A Night In A Dormitory*, one of a series of Melody Comedies churned out by director Harry Delmar. She also appeared briefly in the first of a series of shorts called *Hollywood on Parade*.

The films were made at Paramount's premises at Long Island, hurriedly reconstructed to be able to make talkies. Jesse Lasky, in his book *I Blow My Own Horn*, proudly names Ginger as one of the stars whose careers he helped to start, develop and bring to public acclaim. Mr. Lasky, I feel, was writing with hindsight.

Elsewhere in his book he takes a gloomier view, not so much of Ginger but of the one-reel sound shorts that were then being churned out at Long Island. Lasky writes: 'Our one-reel sound shorts were accepted with apathy because the names of the performers didn't mean anything to cinema audiences— Ethel Merman, Burns & Allen, Ginger Rogers, Charles Ruggles, George Jessel, Willie and Eugene Howard, Jacky Benny, Eddie Cantor, Lillian Roth, Rudy Vallee, Ruth Etting, Gilda Gray and Harry Richman, among others.'

Lasky may have been right at the time; but all these names

made the grade. Jack Benny, George Jessel, George Burns, Ethel Merman, Rudy Vallee and, of course, the redhead from Independence are still operating most successfully. Ginger told me once: 'I don't remember much about those early shorts, except that they gave me an exciting feel of the studios and of the urgency and teamwork needed to make a film—any film.'

Her first real chance was in that year of 1930, with a picture called *Young Man of Manhattan*. This was a *feature* film, and the start of her 73-film career. Ginger was not the star. The 'draw' name in the cast, which also included Norman Foster and Charles Ruggles, was Claudette Colbert, the fascinating, dewy-eyed, soft-smiled, elegant Frenchwoman who had already made three or four feature films for Paramount.

But Ginger had an effective part in this routine newspaper film. She was cast as a wisecracking flapper. She had a song called 'I've Got IT But IT Don't Do Me Any Good' and, more important, a catchphrase, 'Cigarette Me, Big Boy!' Since Ginger is a determined non-smoker, this was ironic. But the tag caught on and for quite a while taxi drivers and people who recognized her on the subway would chortle and fling the catchphrase at her.

Ginger remembers this, her first real film, for another reason. It happens often in film and stage productions but it was a traumatic experience for the inexperienced young Rogers. She was a firm friend of Claudette Colbert, but in the film she had to make love to Norman Foster, who was Claudette's real-life husband at the time. 'I felt terrible at first when I approached these scenes,' admits Ginger. It did not take long to get over the fixation. I mentioned this recently to a producer of one of the modern, permissive, 'anything-goes' films. He looked at me as if I were having him on. Then he said: 'Oh, boy. If we had to worry now about who was married to whom, or who was going to bed with which actress, we'd never even get a film cast!' *Young Man Of Manhattan* launched Ginger as a lively, perky young actress with a nice line in putting over dialogue.

Ginger's own reaction when she saw the finished film was 'My stomach did a complete loop and I wanted to do the picture all over again'.

Young Man Of Manhattan was followed by four other pictures, and you have to be a keen Ginger Rogers fan to recall any of them. *Queen High* found Ginger merely in the background, registering, because of her effervescence, but of little interest in the plot of a tiny story directed by Fred Newmeyer. Charlie Ruggles and Frank Morgan played partners in a garter business. For reasons known only to them and/or the scriptwriters they drew cards to decide which of the two should act as butler to the other for a year. It would be nice to be able to tell you which drew the higher card. But does anybody care? Sufficient that Ginger was a film nearer the stardom which was to be several films and many months ahead.

Other trifles followed. Around this time some of the records say that Ginger made a picture for Paramount Called *Manhattan Mary*, with Ed Wynn. Other records are discreetly silent about what was obviously an exceedingly unimportant non-event. But in *The Sap From Syracuse*, Ginger's shapely torso got plenty of exposure. In this comedy of mistaken identity Jack Oakie apparently spent most of his time chasing her up and down the decks of a liner—and it turned out to be a fairly lively 'she-shanty'.

With *Top Speed* coming to an end, Ginger was beginning to be in demand: a fresh, eager young talent who had got stuck into Broadway and was one to watch, according to the Broadway buzz. Douglas Fairbanks Jr. wanted her for a role in *Reaching For The Moon*. Instead she settled for the musical comedy *Girl Crazy*.

Girl Crazy opened, but Ginger, with her apparently inexhaustible stamina, still made films at Paramount's New York studio. She and Ethel Merman would spend the day filming *Follow The Leader*, in which Ed Wynn starred. It was a routine backstage vehicle for Wynn, with Ginger doing another of her audaciously pert comedy roles as an understudy who replaced a kidnapped Ethel Merman, playing a musical comedy star. It still failed to advance Ginger's film career overmuch, but she was directed by Norman Taurog, an ex-child star of Hollywood, who was later to become a very respected director with his work with children in the *Skippy* films, and many years later, on several films with Elvis Presley.

But the strain of filming all day and being on her peppy toes at night in *Girl Crazy* was taxing. Ginger made only one more film in these circumstances. Then, luckily, she was able to get out before the double stint took too much toll of her health. Her final New York film with Paramount reunited her with Claudette Colbert. It was another routine newspaper film (how very few entertaining *and* authentic ones have ever been made) in which Ginger was cast as the girl friend of reporter Charles Ruggles. The only interesting point about this film is that at last Ginger was working with an entire cast of actresses and actors of obvious class. They were nearly all to have a big future in films and they included (apart from Claudette Colbert and Charles Ruggles) such rising talents as Fredric March, Pat O'Brien, Ralph Morgan and character actor Monroe Owsley. This undistinguished picture was also directed by a woman, a rare thing, for film direction has always largely been a man's world. She was Dorothy Arzner, who had been a film editor before turning to direction with pictures like *Merrily We Go To Hell* and *Nana*. *Honour Among Lovers* may well have been among her last films, for she retired towards the end of the 1930's.

Ginger and her mother sat down and faced the future. It seemed certain that the time was coming when she would have to choose between the theatre and the cinema. The intense double life of 18 hours' work a day could not go on indefinitely without something slipping.

Then, with the folding of *Girl Crazy*, the situation came to a head. Charles R. Rogers, a Pathé producer (who was no relation), offered Ginger a chance of a new life. Before her he dangled the carrot of a contract for Hollywood to make three films. It meant cutting away from the theatre that had become part and parcel of her childhood and adolescence. No more stage-doors. No more footlights. No more audience. No more sound of applause—all that heady stuff that is so enticing to someone who is beginning to make the grade in the theatre.

Yet Hollywood, now fully geared to sound, was an equally enticing challenge. It had become a new world, bursting with enthusiasm, ideas and opportunity for those prepared to work hard and pour in their talent.

For Broadway: It had become their 'home town'. The lights, the delicatessen stores, their friends, the skyline, the subway, Central Park, the Roxy, the local newspapers, Shubert Alley— all these, and many other allurements, were home to Ginger and urged her and her mother to stay where they were quietly starting to plant roots.

For Hollywood: A new atmosphere, the tempting climate, the excitement of mixing in studios with top stars, a well-figured contract, the fact that they were being *invited*.

The decision was difficult. But only for a day or so. Mrs. Rogers' business acumen worked its radar and assured her that Hollywood was where the opportunities were and that they would swell; her mother's instinct assured her that Ginger had the qualifications to cash in on those opportunities. Anyway, they figured, Ginger was not throwing away a lifetime Broadway career. She had made only two appearances in Broadway musicals and, though she had made impact in both, she was not abdicating as the Queen of Broadway. Someone may easily have flung in the practical remark that, if 'flop' was to be the Hollywood result, it took only three days on the Santa Fé railway track to get back to Broadway.

'Hollywood,' said Ginger, 'here I come.'

Ginger's arrival in Hollywood could be termed an 'in-between' event. She was certainly not a 'nobody' coming to try her luck in pictures. On the other hand, she was not a big glamorous name for whose arrival the entire community was waiting with ill-concealed impatience. She moved in quietly, settled down and went to work.

The Depression was still hovering over America like a dank cloud and Ginger could hardly have started a fresh career at a less propitious time, except that she had the confidence of youth and health to back up her ability. The Pathé contract was also a useful insurance over the next couple of years.

She got $1,000 a week for her first Pathé film, *The Tip Off*, but that's about *all* she got out of it. In a radio broadcast in Britain recently her contempt for *Tip Off* was good-humoured but terse. Presumably because she was under contract, Ginger was flung in as comic relief in a fairly glum picture about prize fighting and the underworld, which starred Robert Armstrong and Eddie Quillan.

What does a girl do in a strange country? Honour her contract and hope for the best. The best was going to be quite a while coming.

Robert Armstrong and William Boyd (later to become famous as Hopalong Cassidy) were the stars of Ginger's next chore, *Suicide Fleet*. This one, apparently, involved a mystery ship, and Ginger, on shore, was the target of Armstrong and James Gleason who were rivals against William Boyd for Ginger's affections.

Perhaps I had better make something clear as of this moment. Though a firm cinema buff since the days as a nipper when I sneaked into the Astoria at Seven Kings in Essex to watch people like the early Chaplin and many of the other 'greats', I am not conscious of seeing Ginger Rogers on the screen until about 1932. So any comments here on her earlier films are based simply on hearsay (and we all know how people's memories get hazed), reading, and on the memory of other films with similar titles and similar plots. It seems evident to me that Ginger came up the hard way, doing a professional job in pictures that passed away a few hours in the lives of people to whom the cinema was a novelty and, to very few, a major art.

Carnival Boat, her third picture under her first Hollywood contract, gave the girl from Broadway a chance to show what had excited Broadway audiences. This time she played an entertainer on a carnival boat and had one good song to sing called 'How I Could Go For You'. The plot itself was apparently quite vigorous, with Ginger, the sexy young singer, coming between lumberjack William Boyd and his father Hobart Bosworth. In what way she did so I can only guess. Marie Prevost and Edgar Kennedy, a character actor who became famous as the greatest exponent of the 'slow burn' (a variation of the much more simple 'double take'), also appeared in this now dead and buried piece of celluloid.

It must have been about this time that Ginger and Lela had another career conference. The three-picture contract with Pathé had come to an end and the Rogers team felt that it was time to humour their itching feet. Ginger was now well known as an up-and-coming Hollywood actress, but the three Pathé films had not exactly put her on the star map. A Hollywood columnist I know, who seems to have been around even before some enterprising speculators turned the place into the centre of the film-making world, talked to me about Ginger.

'A darned nice kid' he reminisced over a whisky sour in the Brown Derby. 'Kept her nose clean and herself to herself. Wasn't seen much around the night joints and didn't much seek publicity, but she always co-operated when one wanted to talk with her. But like many of them at the time she was caught up with studio politics. The studios had to make films. They had stars or near-stars under contracts, and the talent was chucked into the films. It wasn't easy for them to argue. Often the films were murder, but the actors had no comeback.'

Ginger's comeback was to seek other fields.

She went to First National for *The Tenderfoot* in which she appeared with Joe E. Brown. Like most Joe E. Brown films the

47

script was geared to the wide-mouthed clown, but Ginger had a role in which she was able to make an impression. She played a typist who saved the gormless cowboy, played by Joe E., from being swindled and as a reward she starred in a show which he eventually produced.

Ginger was now freelancing and she moved to Monogram for her next picture, *The Thirteenth Guest*, a mystery yarn which was another that Ginger, in that BBC radio interview, brushed off with amiable indifference. Yet some of the reviewers found it a 'fair mystery melodrama'. A strange will, a haunted house, a tough detective played by Lyle Talbot, and Ginger as a relative who just escapes being electrocuted, were the chief melodramatic ingredients.

The year 1932 was proving a busy one for a girl who had so recently upsticked and moved from Broadway to tackle the up and down problems of Hollywood. *The Thirteenth Guest* was her fifth Hollywood film that year and there were two still to come. Too many, of course. But at least in those days a would-be star had the chance to keep in tempo, to work with new stars and to be directed and seen by different people. Nowadays, the once-a-yearers can hardly find their way to the studio without a production car, let alone get the smell of their craft.

Next, Ginger was signed for a role in *Hat Check Girl* for Fox, one of the majors. This was the time I lit a match in the cinema darkness to check the name of the girl who was playing Sally Eilers' girl friend. It was, of course, Ginger Rogers.

The film was another one right out of the scriptwriters' sausage machine, with Ben Lyon as a millionaire playboy who became mixed up with cloakroom girl Sally Eilers. Blackmail, of course, reared its platitudinous, but still cinema-intriguing, head. Sally and Ben had all the 'fat' in this film, but I still distantly recall the impact of Ginger, who made a sizeable amount of a cardboard role.

It was back to Joe E. Brown at First National for her next film, *You Said A Mouthful*, in which Ginger was still stooging for

(*above*) Ginger the child with a smile that was to help her to stardom (*below*) With Lela Rogers, the mother who helped her on the road

Princess Alexandra greets Ginger at one of the starry previews of *Mame* at Drury Lane Theatre

Always an outdoor girl, Ginger
is a topline shot and a
near-champion tennis player

In *Hello, Dolly!* (*left*) and
(*above*) as the Bohemian
aunt in *Mame*, two of
Ginger's big stage triump

Hollywood beckons

the star but, by now, doing it with one eye on the crown herself. The amiable gormless comedian invented a nutty swim suit, calculated to make swimming easy. Ginger played a Canadian swimming champion (no problem, for she is a fine swimmer herself) who mistook him for a champ and inveigled him into an important swimming race. The film hardly made a splash, but it was by now the twelfth feature-film credit of a girl who, only two or three years before, had been a completely unknown dancer-singer on a variety circuit.

Ginger could look back on her Hollywood career, with seven films under her graceful belt and some biggish names among her co-players, in the fair belief that her exit from Broadway hadn't simply been a whim. It was quietly working out.

Chapter 4

FIRST STEPS WITH ASTAIRE

The year 1933 was to be Ginger Rogers' most industrious in terms of films made. She appeared in nine films, which is something quite fantastic.

It is true that a star, even when making a movie, gets the occasional day off when he can go fishing, watch sport, sleep or simply sit by a lavish swimpool. But there are also lines to learn during the evenings; early nights, because those 'one-for-the road' lines show up roughly under a camera's clinical, baleful eye; early starts at the studio for make-up; a lot of tiring hanging around while technical problems are solved; publicity interviews; talks with agent and accountants. Oh yes, and a few minutes, occasionally, ought to be devoted to the family. It is no easy life—and nine films is no slacker's programme.

I sometimes think that the main advantage of being a film star is the money. Then, of course, there's the income-tax man waiting to bite.

Even though Ginger was not then a big star it defeats me how she managed to get through such a year of work. It was wise that she did; it brought her some films that gave her breaks and led to others which made all the past work worth it. It was also, within a year or so, to bring her to her second marriage.

It is probably summed up by Ginger's philosophy: 'I like to use every minute of every day purposefully; even when I lounge it is because I believe it helps me to get the best out of my next spell of activity.' I agree with every word she says. I only wish I could do it.

Ginger was working hard, but far from becoming a recluse. In Hollywood there were too many pleasant, healthy escorts around for an equally pleasant and healthy girl not to have plenty of dates. Around this time Ginger was showing up at some of the parties and occasional night spots with a personable director named Mervyn Le Roy. They frequently visited Bebe Daniels and Ben Lyon at their beach home at nearby Santa Monica. 'They seemed very attached to each other,' Ben told me. 'In fact, we thought they might very well marry. It might have been a good thing if they had done so. Anyway, Mervyn was certainly a great help to her career at that time with his encouragement and his savvy.'

It was Le Roy who urged her to say 'O.K.' to a chance of appearing in a Warner musical called *Forty Second Street*. It was to be directed by Lloyd Bacon, and Ginger had already worked with him in a Joe E. Brown comedy, *You Said A Mouthful*. Earlier Bacon had made *The Singing Fool*, the first film with dialogue, and afterwards he had a long career making brightly competent but not outstanding programme films, without ever hitting the high spots.

Ginger realized that she would be in good hands. She could learn much from a capable director like Bacon. She mournfully says: 'I once had a director who I think was illiterate. Anyway, he never seemed able to take in the words of a script.'

Le Roy insisted that *Forty Second Street* could be a useful break for her. The rest of the cast appealed to Ginger too. They were all good working professionals—people like Warner Baxter, George Brent, Bebe Daniels, Una Merkel, Guy Kibbee, Ruby Keeler and Dick Powell. She figured that it might not turn out to be the best picture of the year, but it could hardly be ignored. It wasn't. It turned out to be quite a hit.

Busby Berkeley, then the most noted film dance director in the business, surpassed himself with some dazzling if eccentric dance routines. The songs were cheerful. Bebe Daniels set the film going with 'You're Getting To Be A Habit With Me'. Another that has stood the test of three decades was Al Dubin and Harry Warren's frisky 'Shuffle Off To Buffalo'.

Ginger was perhaps slightly disappointed that she was given no solo musical spot in this peppy, wisecracking backstage film. She and Una Merkel did sing a bit of 'Shuffle Off To Buffalo' but the song was really designed as a Keeler-Powell duet.

The scriptwriter did not need a fertile imagination to dream up the basic storyline; nowadays it could be done by a computer. It was that 'oldie' about a leading lady who, just as the curtain is about to rise on her first night, has an accident and cannot appear. Who should pop up (Surprise! Surprise!) but an unknown, aspiring young actress who happens to be word-perfect and, of course, becomes a star.

Fortunately, Ginger was not saddled with this bewhiskered role. She was cast as a gold-digging dancer and seemed to be around whenever the wisecracks were stirred up: Ginger was becoming adept at tossing off a quip with a slightly acid flavour. She played Anytime Annie, a self-explanatory description. I shall long remember the laughter that greeted a line which, though obvious, is still extremely funny in my view. Someone remarked of Anytime Annie that she only said 'No' once—and that was when she didn't hear the question.

Warner Baxter had a tailored role as a producer who defied his doctor's orders to put on his lavish show. 'I've got to put my show on to make enough money to pay the doctor's bills if I get ill putting on the show,' said Baxter, with a wry logic. With Dick Powell and Ruby Keeler also in the cast Ginger was in first-rate musical comedy company. When the film was ended Ginger was on top of the world and could confidently echo one of its liveliest songs, 'I'm Young And Healthy.' She was to need all her health to cope with her programme for 1933, which was to turn out so busy that it would make 1932 seem almost like a lazy weekend in the country.

First steps with Astaire

Before *Forty Second Street* was released and the useful impact of her slick, wisecracking Anytime Annie was realized, she had been snapped up by Fox for a film called *Broadway Bad*. Her journey from Burbank was hardly necessary. The film was a piece of nothing, in which, once again, Ginger played a chorus girl (she would have to watch that type-casting), this time in support of Joan Blondell, then the Hollywood queen of Ginger's particular type of brittle, amusing comedy. The film was designed so that Joan wrapped it up securely for herself.

It can happen that a director urges an actress into another film to give her more experience and then decides to use her in his own movie. Mervyn Le Roy's urging of Ginger, who was still his current date, to go into *Forty Second Street* was shrewd. A couple of films later Ginger was back at the Warner studios in Le Roy's *Gold Diggers of 1933*. Le Roy had assembled some old chums for this brittle, lusciously designed film (settings by Busby Berkeley, naturally!) which bristled with bright, light-weight patter.

Apart from Ginger, he had signed up a number of 'Warner reliables', talented people like Joan Blondell, Aline MacMahon and the inevitable Ruby Keeler and Dick Powell. There was Warren William as a classy star name, and Le Roy also brought in chubby Guy Kibbee and the wonderful, lugubrious, cigar-smoking Ned Sparks. Sparks with his icy eyes, thin, gloomy face and tight lips, always looked as if he were about to take on the United Nations—irrespective of provocation.

But somehow the picture didn't quite come off. It had some very good moments and Ginger probably captured one of the best. She virtually opened the film, which was about four girls on their beam ends waiting for some rich Prince Charming (Dick Powell, who else?) to finance a Broadway show for them. Ginger, wearing a breath-taking gown smothered with gold coins, appeared on the screen singing 'We're In The Money'. She looked like a nympho advert for the Bank of America and made a huge impression. There were several other good scenes in this frisky lark, including Dick Powell and Ruby Keeler trying to sing 'Petting In The Park' with incongruous interruptions from an odd little dwarf, and a flashy, momentarily effective Busby Berkeley dance scena called the Shadow Waltz.

But still the picture didn't entirely click. It was bitty and at times banal. Yet if you mention it to anyone old enough to have seen it (which probably cuts out anybody under the age of, say, fifty) they will remember Ginger singing 'We're In The Money'. It is from such moments that a film career can be created.

Ginger and her mother were still diligently exploring outlets for Ginger's future. Lela was bargaining constantly with other studios, but it was to be five films later before a minor, unexpected but highly useful explosion occurred. Five more films. It seems formidable, but in those days pictures were turned out far more quickly. Nowadays, most studios are cautious and almost ludicrously unimaginative. They invariably wait till someone writes a book or a play and if the public turns it into a best seller or a long running West End or Broadway success *then* they bring out their cheque books. By the time a property is negotiated, bought, written as a screenplay, rewritten, blown up as a hard-ticket extravaganza, frequently retitled, cast, shot, processed and released, two or three years can have passed. Films are now so expensive to make that companies cannot risk taking too many reckless chances.

Ginger's break, though it took five films to come off, happened in that same busy year of 1933. Her schedule was giving her little chance to do anything except zoom from studio to studio, which was fine at the time for the ambitious youngster. For her next picture she moved over to the RKO-Radio studio which, though she did not know it then, was to become her Tom Tiddler's ground for many years.

The film was *Professional Sweetheart*, and it was a disaster. The idea was to poke fun at radio but it lacked wit, subtlety or satire and sagged throughout like a damp deckchair. Ginger was cast as 'The Purity Girl Of The Air'. What a tag! If Ginger had had the inclination or the time in those busy months of 1933 no one could have blamed her for hitting the town and providing the local columnists with heaven-sent headlines— 'Purity Girl Rogers Peps It Up At The Pep Spots'.

Ginger played it cool and got on with the job of playing 'The Purity Girl Of The Air' in the film, in which she had to select Norman Foster as her Dream Man and then shock him. The only people really shocked were those at the box offices waiting to take the diffident public's money.

Looking back, it is interesting to see how a potential talent and box-office draw was idly wasted in those days The freelance actress, like Ginger, was in a tight spot: caught both ways. Under studio contract she could have been flung into any film to earn her weekly pay packet. As a freelance, however, she was not much better off. The meaty, effective roles were naturally handed to the studio's name stars. The freelance was likely to get only the 'left-overs'. But Ginger, who talked the problem over with her mother, was still convinced that some day the lone wolf attitude would pay dividends.

Meanwhile the two lived quietly and unostentatiously in this glittering ambience of dream mansions, shimmering swimming pools and crazy entertaining. Ginger just trundled from studio to studio, wherever the next chance cropped up.

She made three more pedestrian pictures. They were mostly trashy, but served their purpose in that they drew local customers into cinemas at a time when there were no counter-attractions such as television or bingo. Does anybody now recall *A Shriek In The Night*? Ginger played a newspaper reporter who, in competition with another reporter, Lyle Talbot, was trying to break a murder story. All in the course of newspaper (and film) duty Ginger was nearly burned to death on screen in a blazing furnace.

A Shriek In The Night having simmered down to a completely inaudible whimper, Ginger turned to Universal studios, which cast her in *Don't Bet On Love*. In this she turned up as a manicurist who spent most of her time trying to reform her boy friend, a plumber who could not be lured from the race track. This was yet another film which did little or nothing to veer Ginger towards her inevitable stardom, but it had an important effect on the private life of the busy, still reserved girl from Broadway. The leading man was Lew Ayres.

Lew, two or three years older than Ginger, had been a musician whose job led him to Hollywood and an engagement at the Coconut Grove night spot with Ray West's band. Though he was a skilled performer on the piano, guitar and banjo he was drawn to acting. He became an extra, got a small role in a Pathé picture called *Condemned* and a short contract. Then he played in *The Kiss* with Garbo, a very nice start for an aspiring young actor. But it was his performance in *All Quiet On The Western Front*, Lewis Milestone's epic war film, that started him off on an acting career which has had a full quota of ups and downs. Ayres had the misfortune of many actors. His first newsworthy and critically acclaimed performance was always flaunted in front of him; everything he did later was compared—usually unfavourably. He didn't stand a chance when, years later, he went through a routine, but perfectly competent, series of mild adventures as Dr. Kildare showing life in a hospital. Unfortunately, neither Erich Maria Remarque, who wrote *All Quiet On The Western Front*, nor director Lewis Milestone was around to work on *Dr. Kildare*.

But this sensitive, well-read young actor and the slowly rising young actress, Ginger Rogers, struck up an immediate friendship and soon the Hollywood gossip writers were at work. Their busy little typewriters started to rattle when the two were seen having quiet dinners or an occasional dance at a night spot. They hinted at an impending romance, and for once their guesswork was to turn out to be true.

Meanwhile, Ginger was still happily busy and in demand at studios. Her agent was certainly diligent on her behalf. Paramount, the company which had first launched her in minor films, beckoned, and Ginger found herself in *Sitting Pretty*. Though the film itself was yet another nondescript affair, a piece of whipped-up malarkey in which Ginger played a singing and dancing café owner who joined up with a couple of song-writers in search of glamorous Hollywood fame, she was working with some artists who were beginning to forge ahead in pictures. She joined up again, for instance, with that dimply bovine-faced comedian Jack Oakie, with whom she'd played in *The Sap From Syracuse* at Paramount's New York studio. There were also Jack Haley, the irascible Gregory Ratoff, Lew Cody, most suave and debonair of screen villains, and Thelma Todd, a striking blonde who committed suicide under the strain and pressures of Hollywood stardom. Ginger had two or three songs, probably by Harry Revel, who appeared in the film as a song-writer. Thank heaven, I can't remember them even in my bath, but Ginger scored heavily with one gaily romantic song which I still remember with pleasure. It was 'Did You Ever See A Dream Walking?'

Ginger was settling down comfortably in Hollywood. She was swiftly mastering the screen technique and studios were conscious of her charm, talent and vivacity and were wanting her for their films. She had plenty of work and enough friends. Yet her eager ego felt that she was not yet making the progress she should.

She wondered why. Ginger was not aware of it, but her next film was to be the pusher—the one that was to open the door to a career of worldwide success. Meanwhile, she had to be content with winning an award *d'estime*. She was named a 'Wampus Baby Star of 1932' and though it may have given her a slight sense of exhilaration at the time—well, madam, if you were 21, eager and ambitious, how would *you* care to be known as a 'Wampus Baby'?

In fact, it was a highly useful accolade, despite the curious title. The Wampus Baby Stars for each year were picked by Californian newspapermen as the girls most likely to reach stardom. Naturally, the newspapermen were hard behind their selections and gave them all the publicity and push they could. The newspapermen did a good job of crystal-gazing in 1932; most of their 14 selections made the grade and any keen film follower will recognize the names of at least half of them, though that of Ginger Rogers has certainly turned out to be the biggest and most enduring.

Gloria Stuart, Lilian Bond, Mary Carlisle and Boots Mallory, the Broadway stage showgirl who married that most English of Englishmen, Herbert Marshall, Evalyn Knapp, Dorothy Wilson and Eleanor Holm, the swimming champion, were among the selections and achieved some success. I am afraid I don't know much about what happened to Toshia Mori, Ruth Hall, Patricia Ellis, Marian Shockley, Dorothy Layton and Lona Andre. They probably had their little day, their flirtation with fame, and then settled for marriage or other careers.

But 37 years later Ginger Rogers, ex-Wampus Baby of 1932, is still in the front rank.

In her New York days—already they seemed light years ago —Ginger had come to know Fred Astaire quite well on a friendly basis. She had met him when Herbert Ross, the brilliantly eccentric editor of the *New Yorker*, had taken her backstage to see Fred while his name was in glowing lights over Broadway.

They had dated, casually, a few times: the odd dinner, the occasional movie, some rare nights when they had danced at the Central Park Casino dance hall. But neither had ever dreamed that one day they would dance their way into the hearts of millions of people the world over. Portly men with two left feet would be getting a vicarious kick out of trying to emulate the immaculate trick steps of Fred (who, incidentally, is not, I gather from several Hollywood stars, a particularly good ballroom dancer) and from imagining themselves with

Ginger in their arms; their partners would get an equally vicarious thrill by imagining that they had the sinuous grace of Miss Rogers.

The two would sit around the Rogers apartment and, with Lela, discuss their hopeful futures. It never remotely occurred to either of them that those futures would, for a few brief, magnetic years, be so entwined. Who would then have predicted that the names of Astaire and Rogers as a team would become as easy on the tongue as Swan and Edgar, Marks and Spencer, Laurel and Hardy, Fortnum and Mason, and Burton and Taylor?

Thornton Freeland, who was to direct *Flying Down To Rio*, told me years later, while we were sipping drinks contentedly over the bar of Siegi Sessler's Club in Mayfair: 'I knew we had a lot of good things going for us. The leading lady was that dark-haired charmer Dolores Del Rio, one of the most beautiful women ever to be in films. The leading man was Gene Raymond, blonde, virile, good-looking. And there were cast-iron supporting actors like Franklyn Pangborn, with his pained, downtrodden air of outraged dignity, and Eric Blore.

'All right', continued Freeland, 'the storyline was a shade slim but in those days nobody cared much about the story in a musical. We had music by Vincent Youmans—and that was an asset, anyway.'

They also had Fred Astaire and Ginger Rogers. 'They were quite electrifying,' Thornton told me, 'and, of course, they eventually became the talking point of the film.'

Astaire, a big name on the stage, had been lured to Hollywood to make a film called *Dancing Lady* with Joan Crawford, and, though as bewildered and nervous as an apprentice jockey riding in his first Grand National, he had acquitted himself extremely well.

For Fred it was like Old Home Week when he found that he was to dance with Ginger. He liked Hollywood and was excited about the chance of getting a foothold in what was to him a new medium. But he knew he had a lot to learn. Ginger, in her packed two years, had become something of a veteran in studio and screen technique. Maybe the full result had not yet been seen on the screen, but she knew the tricks and the pitfalls that lingered both before and behind the cameras. She helped Fred dodge a lot of them.

They shared something ironical in common, details of film tests which may even now be gathering dust in filing cabinets in Hollywood and causing hot flushes to the people who inspired them if ever they will admit it. Fred's was downright insulting as to his physical allure and acting ability, though the card grudgingly admitted that he could dance a bit. Ginger had only recently emerged from a screen test and had not come out unscathed.

Harry Cohn, the shrewd but ruthlessly egotistical boss of Columbia Pictures, wanted to sign up Ginger on a long term contract for his company. He had seen several of her films (and some of them, frankly, were drivel), but though Ginger stood out all the way as obvious star material Cohn could not quite make up his mind whether to risk signing her up on a long term contract.

He decided on a test. Then he made the fatal error of showing it at his home to a friendly rival named Merian Cooper, top tycoon at RKO.

Cooper saw the test and groaned inwardly. This was disaster; but he too was shrewd enough to realize that the girl had an abundance of talent. He phoned Lela Rogers and said, without any preamble: 'Lela, last night, at Harry Cohn's place, I saw the worst test I have ever clapped eyes on. . . .'

Lela knew what he was getting at, but she played along with wily common-sense. 'So?' she said. 'What's that to do with me?' apparently bridling slightly.

'But it was a test of *Ginger*,' Cooper exploded. 'I saw a fresh little girl trying to play a mature woman lawyer. How could you let Harry *do* it?'

Lela let Cooper make the next move. This could be the
moment they had been waiting for.

There was a pause. Then Cooper said: 'Come on over to the
office. I want to talk with you.' The talk went well.

So when Fred Astaire joined up with Ginger in Hollywood
she was a fully fledged star with a contract for seven years.
When Fred and Ginger had enjoyed a few lighthearted dates in
New York he had perhaps jokingly predicted that soon she
would be a movie queen; perhaps she was now on the way.
The seven-year contract extended to 14 years, fraught a bit, no
doubt, but on the whole very amiable and successful. She made
37 films while at RKO including a few for which she was
profitably loaned out to other studios.

During those Tumultuous Thirties before the war she became
an international name. It was Hollywood's champagne era,
when stars and films lifted ordinary folk into a make-believe
world, adding gaiety and colour to their everyday round.
Ginger was rightly glad to be a part of a film era that was none
the worse for not taking itself too seriously or pompously.

One dance launched the famous Fred Astaire-Ginger Rogers
partnership, a whirling ball of a dance called the Carioca.
When the two met at the studio for rehearsal Fred was a bit
apprehensive. Ginge (as he alone is permitted to call her) had
been making straight films since the *Forty Second Street* and *Gold
Diggers* tuners. He wondered how she would feel at reverting to
musicals.

Frankly, she didn't know. She had been contented enough to
keep on with the non-dancing, non-singing pictures. But Fred
recalls in his book *Steps In Time*, her reaction was typical. Said
Ginger: 'I guess it will turn out all right. Anyway, we'll have
fun.' That summed it up. She never minded how much work
was involved, but anything she took on she expected to enjoy
doing. It is still the Rogers philosophy.

Before starting on *Flying Down To Rio* she had just returned
from a location where she had been filming *Chance At Heaven,*

with Joel McCrea and Andy Devine. This was a rather ropy soap-opera, in which Ginger played a small-town girl in love with McCrea. He married, instead, a wealthy debutante, played by Marian Nixon. The scriptwriters on this one hardly extended themselves. The marriage between McCrea and his hard, opulent bride was obviously destined to flop but it did not need a keen student of the cinema to realize that before the fade-out Ginger and Joel would be reunited to the satisfaction of all cinemagoers who still cared.

It was directed by Bill Seiter, who had steered Ginger and Norman Foster, plus the unforgettable Zasu Pitts, through a farrago of nonsense called *Professional Sweetheart*. It probably explains why Ginger welcomed *Flying Down To Rio*, which, flimsy though it might be, did have some zest, pace and fun.

Some of Vincent Youmans' songs for the film were very ear-worthy, such as the title song and 'Orchids In The Moonlight'. Ginger and Fred both had separate song spots and were also together in some of the situations. But it was their dancing together of the Carioca that really gave the film its crescendo. Fred was not too optimistic (but then, I gather from him that he never is about his work). In fact he set off to appear on the London stage in *The Gay Divorce* without even seeing *Rio*, convinced that his film career was prematurely buried.

But while he was basking in his success in London he got a cable from one of RKO's executives, Pandro Berman, which perked him up a great deal. Astaire thought that he would be dreadful in *Rio*. The cable reassured him. Berman said that the preview of the film had been terrific and, shortly afterwards, its opening at the Radio City Music Hall in New York confirmed Berman's enthusiasm.

Fred hadn't realized that he and Ginger dancing the Carioca were going to be a smash hit. Never one to move into superlatives, he cautiously remarks: 'I thought Ginger and I looked all right together, but I never believed that we were doing anything outstanding.'

The audiences thought they were.

The beautiful Dolores Del Rio and Gene Raymond were strong competition, but the Carioca bowed in a new, irresistible team. Ginger was a redhead, of course, but in the film she came out as a delicious, dishy blonde. Astaire was not the conventional hero. Wasn't his hair thinning a little? Where were those male-hero biceps? But somehow the two matched like strawberries and cream or gin-and-Martini. When they danced the Carioca audiences sat up and realized that they were watching a new piece of movie magic.

There was a sudden thrill which one American critic described as 'completely supercharged'. This was not just skilled ballroom dancing. It was the emergence of a new technique created specially and superbly for the screen. The cameras followed them as, with knees, eyes, smiles and feet, the two flirted. It was all done with such a sense of gaiety and amusement. Other dancers might have charged around at an even tempo. But not Astaire and Rogers. They would pause, time the pause to a fraction and then flowingly continue with their glowing, frenzied whirlpools of movement. So smooth, so glib, so right—a mosaic of motion. It was a new form of ecstatic, pulsating love making—and yet only in one film did Ginger and Fred ever even kiss. Their screen romances were the gayest, most platonic, foot-floating flirtations that had ever happened, or have ever happened since. I often wonder what would have happened if the two had become the duet stars now that they were then. The dancing would still have been magic. But this permissive age would surely have demanded that at some time during every film the two would leave the ballroom to writhe, naked, in bed. The magic would have waned. I doubt if in the bygone age of 'innocence' audiences would have stood for such behaviour from this happy-go-lucky, infinitely charming couple. But the idea never arose.

The glamorous Astaire-Rogers partnership was put in cold storage for a time. Ginger went on busily making films, marking up her 1934 output to the industrious number of seven; and she still had time to move into her second marriage.

Following *Rio*, and the obvious certainty that RKO would not contemplate tossing away such an exciting and potentially profitable new star team, William Seiter directed her in *Rafter Romance*. It was no sensation and was obviously one of several fill-ins until the studio could find a smart follow-up for *Flying Down To Rio*, but it teamed Ginger again with her old friend Norman Foster. It also had Robert Benchley in its cast. Benchley, a fine comic writer, must also have been stage-struck. He appeared in many films, usually bumbling his way along, and without stepping too much on the fringe of the plot. I must say that I preferred him as the writer of his short, witty essays.

Rafter Romance was a Box and Cox type of comedy, conscientiously churned out by a scriptwriter who hit on the not brilliant but quite joky idea of Norman Foster as an artist who, to make a living, was a night watchman in the dark hours. He slept in a Greenwich village attic during the day. Ginger occupied it at night—an obvious cue for the flippant complications that cropped up.

While RKO was still trying to decide on a follow-up film for Ginger and Fred Astaire, she was loaned out to a number of other companies. The films were mainly cut-of-the-cloth affairs, now almost forgotten; but they enabled Ginger to play with new artists and be directed by other craftsmen. All the time she was learning her craft.

The next picture for Ginger was *Finishing School* for RKO, in which she played Frances Dee's unruly room-mate in a light-hearted story about a girls' college. The advantage of this film was that one of the cast was Billie Burke, a splendid light comedienne who well repaid close study by Ginger. She then moved across to First National for *Twenty Million Sweethearts*, with Dick Powell and Pat O'Brien.

Ginger was a radio star who had just lost her weekly show.

First steps with Astaire

Dick played a singing waiter, spotted by agent Pat O'Brien and given a big break. But he had mike-fright and Ginger spent most of the film curing the singing waiter's nerves and helping to turn him into a star. I read somewhere that later this was remade with Doris Day and Jack Carson under the title of *My Dream is Yours* but everybody seems very cagy about admitting it; I don't altogether blame them.

This was proving another busy year for Ginger, but though she was turning out the goods in a completely professional way, flimsy stories and routine roles were doing little to advance her career, except for the valuable experience of working and the confidence coming from being in demand. Fox opened up their doors for her next film, *Change of Heart*. This was another piece of pointless froth about two pairs of college graduates who go to New York to find jobs. They find the going tough and predictably end up by changing their partners when romance strikes.

This could not have surprised the audiences too much, for the original pairs were Ginger and Charles Farrell and Janet Gaynor and James Dunn. Janet and Farrell had made a huge romantic success in the silent film *Seventh Heaven* and later in *Sunny Side Up* and *The First Year*. They both made separate pictures but it was as young lovers together that audiences enthused over them. Farrell and Miss Gaynor might well have gone on to become screenland's oldest pair of lovers if Charles Farrell hadn't struck out to become a fashionable club and hotel owner.

The only other minor point of interest in *Change of Heart* was that in the cast was a small girl who was to become a star in *Little Miss Marker*. She was Shirley Temple, the greatest World's Sweetheart since the original Mary Pickford. Now, surprisingly, she is a retired actress taking an active part in American politics and civic affairs, though even her screen reputation has not helped her to make more than a mild ripple in these more turbulent seas.

About this time the Hollywood gossip writers, who can smell out a prospective news item avidly when forced to (or just as avidly invent one when trying to meet a deadline), noted with interest that Ginger was still dating actor Lew Ayres, with whom she had made a film a few months earlier. (He had first seen her at the premiére of *Forty Second Street* and later they met at a studio canteen.)

With three more films on her 1934 plate there was obviously little chance for the romance—if indeed it turned out to be one —to progress at a pace sufficiently indiscreet for the columnists, who like their romantic bits to be quick, unexpected and as colourful as possible. But the newshawks noted that the two were occasionally to be seen dining quietly at Beverly Hills restaurants, and that Lew Ayres occasionally visited Ginger at the exotically tagged Garden of Allah Hotel on Sunset Boulevard, where she and her mother were living at the time. They filed the news for future reference and contented themselves with not-so-veiled hints of the 'Which leading lady and her former leading man are liking to eat where you meet the élite?' variety.

Meanwhile, Ginger was wondering where the real break would come. Back she went to Warner's for a single picture at the studio where she had first been spotted in *Forty Second Street* and *Gold Diggers of 1933*. With Roy Del Ruth directing, Ginger appeared in *Upper World*, in which she played a chorus girl (what, again?) with Warren William, Mary Astor, Andy Devine, little Dickie Moore and J. Carroll Naish. Mary Astor was a society wife, so keen on gadding around that she completely neglected her business-man husband, Warren William. He became involved (fairly innocently, for Ginger's public demanded that she was always a 'nice girl') with the chorus girl, and her employer, J. Carroll Naish, stuck him up for blackmail. I dimly recall this one not only because, not for the first time, I was pondering if I would ever be able to afford such impeccable tailoring as Mr. William's, but because Ginger was killed in the movie. This was the first time (and, I believe, the

66

last) that this vivacious girl was blotted out so sadly on the screen. Mind you, it wasn't premeditated. Naish pulled a gun on Warren William and Ginger gallantly rushed across and blocked out the shot; nevertheless, it made me feel quite wistful for all of a couple of hours after I left the cinema. They really shouldn't bump off our Ginger!

After this rough experience it was back to the haven of her home studio and, with it, the film which was to become a legend and start a several-year cult which even the most egghead cinemaphile does not attempt to knock. *The Gay Divorce* was filmed and the dancing reign of Astaire and Rogers really began after their brisk, successful bow in *Flying Down To Rio*.

In London, at the Palace Theatre, Fred Astaire had made his first stage appearance without his sister, Adèle, but despite her absence *The Gay Divorce* had the audience and the critics in joyful agreement. The musical was a winner. Meanwhile, RKO's Pandro Berman had cabled Fred that *Flying Down To Rio* had opened wonderfully at New York's Radio City Music Hall, that Astaire's RKO contract had been taken up and that Berman was planning to come to London to see *The Gay Divorce*.

Obviously, if Berman liked it *The Gay Divorce* would be Fred's next film. It was also almost certain, after *Rio*, that Ginger and he would be teamed again. RKO knew that in the pair they had a winner; even RKO could not have known that eventually the Astaire-Rogers musicals would gross spectacular millions of dollars at the box-office.

When the show ended in London and Fred returned to California the anticipated plan started rolling. The title was to be altered to *The Gay Divorcee*. Since the plot hinged on Ginger's 'divorce' it seemed a more glamorous and apt title. (In Britain, however, the original title was retained.) To give Fred more scope, he was to play a dancer instead of a writer, as in the stage version. Ginger was happy at being drawn back into what she thought would be 'the odd musical' probably not expecting that, for several years, the musicals were to put her straight acting aspirations somewhat in the background.

Only one of Cole Porter's *Gay Divorce* songs was retained and that was the haunting, rhythmic, never-to-be-forgotten 'Night and Day'; but there were wonderful ear- and eye-worthy additions. Eric Blore, with his bland voice and characteristic walk and smile, was in the cast as the inevitable and definitive butler-cum-valet. So were sleek Erik Rhodes and the perpetually worried and nervous Edward Everett Horton. Adding to the glamour was Betty Grable, a blonde playing her first worth-while role, who was to become a big star and whose legs were to produce photographs that excited impressionable young men so much that in the war a few years later she was to be the No. 1 Pin Up Girl.

The story was as slight as a chorus girl's waist. Edward Everett Horton, a lawyer acting for Ginger in her pending divorce, fixed for her to go to a hotel and meet Erik Rhodes, a professional co-respondent hired by the conniving Horton. The complications came fast and furiously when, at the hotel, she was introduced to dancer Astaire, who got entirely the wrong idea of what was happening and fell for her with a thump, with the usual musicomedy misunderstandings.

Ginger had a good song called 'Don't Let It Bother You', Fred found himself musically 'Looking For A Needle In A Haystack' and Horton and Betty Grable both scored in a duet called 'Let's K-k-nock K-nees'. And there were two spectacular dance scenes which lifted audiences from their seats with delight and did much towards steering the Astaire-Rogers team to fame.

One was the 'Night and Day' duet. The other was the lavish, exciting, whirling Continental, written by Herb Magidson and Con Conrad and with the subtle Hermes Pan dancing direction to add to Astaire's inventiveness. It had the same effect, perhaps more so, as the flying Carioca in *Flying Down To Rio*.

The steps of 'Night and Day' spoke eloquently with its throbbing rhythm and intensely romantic lyric:

First steps with Astaire

'Night and day, you are the one,
Only you beneath the moon and under the sun.
Whether near to me or far,
It's no matter, darling, where you are,
I think of you,
Night and day. . . .'

Fred was in no two minds about his feelings for Ginger in this great song; she was not so sure. He lured her to him in the dance, she pushed him away, but he wouldn't be denied and as the dance ended and Ginger sank back on to a sofa they looked at each other. Ginger was melting and there was no doubt that she was conquered. No words can really do justice to the exhilaration of that scene and the blending of dancing limbs fully attuned.

The Continental folded up the film in a speedy, tingling mass of dancers, with Fred and Ginger naturally dominating it, and helped tremendously by swift, imaginative cutting and sparkling camera work. Their gay exit from the hotel ballroom could hardly have been better designed to make their admirers long impatiently for their next film. It was to come the following year, and quickly on the heels of *The Gay Divorcee*.

But Ginger was scheduled for one more film that year, an unexciting, bathetic potboiler called *Romance In Manhattan*, with Ginger falling in love with a handsome Czech immigrant (Francis Lederer) who is out of work, out of luck and out of spirits. The last two hardships were shared by most who saw it.

It was about this time, in November 1934, that the Hollywood columnists' patience was rewarded. Ginger made her second attempt to find permanence in married happiness. A few years before, when Eddie Cantor wanted Florenz Ziegfeld to sign her for a show at the Oriental Theatre, Chicago, the 'glorifier of beautiful women' had not apparently been over impressed by Ginger's wholesome but not voluptuous charms. He had said kindly and jokingly: 'Go and nab yourself a rich husband.'

Lew Ayres was certainly not rich, but he looked to have a bright future as a Hollywood actor. He had come to Hollywood as a singer and musician and after a spell with dance bands his lissom, youthful good looks had attracted the film people who had offered him some extra work and then one or two bit parts, which he had taken in a spirit of 'What have I got to lose?'

Came *All Quiet On The Western Front* and the opening up of an acting future for Ayres. He and Ginger had made the film *Don't Bet on Love* together; for the second time Ginger was to find out that you cannot do that with any confidence.

The two were married on a November day at the Little Church of the Flowers and her cousin Phyllis Fraser, Mary Brian, the actress who was the screen Peter Pan, and Janet Gaynor, a friend of Ginger's since they had filmed together in *Change Of Heart*, were her matrons of honour. Ginger, now fast becoming a big name in films, held the reception at the Ambassadors Hotel and it was attended by many of Hollywood's upper crust.

But the happy pair were not very impressed. Their first date had been at a theatre at a time of local earthquake rumbles. Scared, Ginger had asked Lew to duck the theatre and they went off to play table-tennis instead. Just as coolly and nonchalantly the bride and bridegroom did the minimum of honours at the reception and swiftly skipped away. They disappeared in a Buick coupé, which Lew had given Ginger as an engagement present, and instead of playing host and hostess might have been found some distance away, still in their wedding finery, vigorously enjoying a session in a bowling alley!

Just what went wrong with the marriage only Ginger or Lew can say. It lasted barely a couple of years, though the divorce was left till much later. The Hollywood grapevine buzzed and said that, for the second time, Lela Rogers had not approved of her daughter marrying at this early stage in her career. The gossips clacked and suggested that though Lew was only three years older than his young wife, he was infinitely more mature,

70

and that Ginger was really seeking a 'father figure' rather than a husband. Ginger scoffed at this, saying: 'I hardly knew my real father. I liked my stepfather a great deal but never saw him after he divorced my mother. So why would I need a father figure?'

Maybe she wasn't really looking for a husband either?

Ginger had left hotel life behind her and was living in her first Hollywood home. She had done the merry-go-round of parties as soon as she had begun to make an impact in Hollywood. Now, happy in her new marriage and conscious that the studio lights and the social bright lights didn't mix for a hard-working, conscientious young actress, she was content to live almost the life of a recluse with Lew.

In their first year of marriage they went to no parties and rarely entertained, preferring to go out occasionally to a restaurant for a quiet dinner. Ginger admits that this was partly because, in those days, anyway, she wasn't much of a cook. 'I even managed to get lumps in gravy,' she says.

Her husband spent a lot of time at home studying astronomy (teaching the eagerly receptive Ginger a great deal about his hobby), and Ginger was happy to listen to records or the radio, read and start to dabble with the drawing and painting which was to become an essential pastime. Nowadays, it is practically an obsession; combined with acting it fulfils most of her artistic needs.

She would swim, play tennis and go out with her friends, Phyllis Fraser and Janet Gaynor. They'd go downtown and slip into unexpected cinemas where they saw some splendidly terrible films. 'I just love awful movies,' Ginger will tell you. Maybe it is a slight guilt complex, for she has appeared in some fairly gruesome movies herself; now, however, she can see other people's film lapses on television.

Perhaps eventually Ginger's boundless energy and capacity for life and living began to clash with Lew's more introspective, quieter attitude. All her previous husbands have chivalrously but firmly agreed that 'Ginger's a hard one to keep up with and she insists that you do'. Perhaps that is why her second marriage began to feel the strain?

Anyway, it was time for the actress to go back to work. She aimed to consolidate her fast rising career. She had no *All Quiet On The Western Front* laurels on which to rest. At least, not then.

Chapter 5

THE SONG AND DANCE SAGA

The three films in which William Seiter had previously directed Ginger had not exactly been sensations, but you never know when lightning's going to strike. *Roberta*, RKO's choice as a follow up to *The Gay Divorcee*, was to turn out smoothly, elegantly and satisfyingly. In addition to the stars, Fred, Ginger, Irene Dunne, Helen Westley and others, including Lucille Ball, the picture was to have special woman's appeal because it centred around the world of fashion.

The rich and powerful television executive Lucille Ball, also the zany comedienne of the small screen, is said to have been a discovery of Lela Rogers. Naturally, when Ginger had taken up 'residence' at RKO on long-term contract, her manager-cum-adviser-cum-protector, her mother, had moved in as well. It is said that, partly to make use of Mrs. Rogers' astute knowledge of the business but also to keep her away from her daughter long enough for Ginger to get through the day's work, RKO had appointed Lela as talent scout and coach.

It was a shrewd move, for this experienced woman knew her stuff. At her acting school in the RKO studios she discovered or developed the talents of such artists as Jack Carson and Tyrone Power, to name but two. As Head of New Talent she was an acquisition to the studio, and the Rogers twosome were working under the same roof.

Roberta, many years later to be remade by Metro-Goldwyn-Mayer as *Lovely To Look At*, with Kathryn Grayson and Howard

Keel, had everything going for it as a super, lavish musical. As usual, no one worried over much about the plot of a musical.

Bob Hope had played the Astaire role on the stage and the film had to do with a Paris dress designer's seasonal presentation, with dirty work by his rivals. Ginger played a bogus countess. No, the plot didn't amount to much; but the stars were attractive and confidently pleased with their material and at playing together; the settings were sumptuous; the gowns vivid, fashionable and extravagant enough to make every woman's eyes pop with envy. I'll always recall a gown of glittering gold metal leaf cloth worn by Ginger. Above all, the dress parade which was the film's climax was in colour, then a comparative novelty, and it was rich and rewarding. It revealed Ginger's hair as by no means a fiery red but a soft, fair auburn and at the sight of it her male fans in the cinemas should have renewed their marital vows.

Above all, though, *Roberta* was noteworthy for its music. RKO had no intention of skimping on this. Cole Porter had set the standard with *Divorcee*; later the Gershwins and Irving Berlin were to write for the Astaire-Rogers films. *Roberta* called on that master melodist Jerome Kern, with such slick, sophisticated lyricists as Jimmy McHugh, Oscar Hammerstein II, Otto Harbach and Dorothy Fields—and you can't ask for a better nap hand than that.

'I Won't Dance' (Don't Ask Me), 'Let's Begin', 'Yesterdays' and those three brilliant songs, 'Lovely To Look At', 'The Touch Of Your Hand' and 'Smoke Gets In Your Eyes' made up a score which, interspersed between the clauses, would make even an income-tax demand sound entertaining. *The Times* noted that the dancing 'had more of the ballet than the ballroom about it'.

With *Roberta* finished, the team were firmly established and, for their musical and dancing numbers at least, they had already reached the stage where direction was hardly necessary once the slogging weeks of rehearsals were behind them. Some-

one said: 'All you really need to do is to point the camera at
Fred and Ginger and they'll take it from there.' Of course, it
was never quite as simple as that, but the two quickly developed
a style and an instinct by which they were always very much
aware and in command of the effect that would be screened.

Meanwhile, until the next musical was planned, Ginger was
cast with that most knowing and burnished of stars, William
Powell, and such deft supporting actors as Frank Morgan,
Gene Lockhart, Leslie Fenton and Paul Kelly, in *Star of
Midnight*. Whether or not it was that Ginger's professional star
was in the ascendant, whether it was luck or whether the studio
bosses were taking more care of their precious investment I
would not know. But this turned out to be a better-than-average
whodunit—sophisticated, witty and spirited—in which William
Powell, as a sleuth, and Ginger, as a beautiful society girl,
stylishly solved a tricky crime.

Then it was announced that the next Astaire-Rogers fun-
musical, with music by Irving Berlin, was to be *Top Hat*.
Unfortunately, Ginger's domestic life was by no means as
blissful as life in the studio. It was, it seems, in a state of
unhostile incompatibility. At the end of the year she and Lew
Ayres were to separate and Ginger was to pay him this tribute:
'Lew's a very nice man and a brilliant fellow, but like so many
who are introverts he does not show his true brilliance. He has
written books, plays and even symphonic music—but somehow
you would never realize it.'

Top Hat was to reunite the pair with Mark Sandrich, who
had got them away to a great start when he directed them in
The Gay Divorcee. It was a happy omen. Fred and Ginger also
had with them the inevitable Eric Blore, Eric Rhodes, Edward
Everett Horton and Lucille Ball, and they must have begun to
feel rather like a repertory company. There was also that
astringent actress Helen Broderick with the voice that could be
highly tart when she had what one critic called a few dry
Martini lines to say.

Top Hat, arguably, turned out to be the finest of all the Astaire-Rogers entertainments. It has been shown several times on television and though it loses some sparkle on the small screen it persistently revives memories for the middle-aged. Perhaps more remarkably, it also invariably enchants the younger generation which so often has a genuine admiration for things past. The only real criticism I have read of this musical was in the *Daily Telegraph*, whose critic 'hated Ginger's clothes'.

The film still has a gaiety and swing which have not aged, just as nothing can wither the dancing delight of Ginger and Fred in their prime. Once again there's little need to labour the contrived story, a slight yet complicated taradiddle about mixed-up love, plotting and mistaken identity, with everybody jumping to convenient if wrong conclusions and everything being sorted out to the satisfaction, at least, of the hero and heroine. Many a film with similar ingredients has passed an hour or so away without the advantages that put *Top Hat* high up among light screen fare.

Fred is a dancing musical comedy star, Horton a producer, Erik Rhodes a gown designer and Ginger the employee who models his gowns at the swish parties which she attends: about all one needs to know regarding the book of a musical show. To me the best song in the film is Berlin's cheeky yet gently sentimental 'Isn't This A Lovely Day To Be Caught In The Rain'', sung and danced by the deft-footed stars in a park bandstand in stormy weather. Yet each of the songs matched the mood needed by the lighthearted picture at any given moment. Fred singing 'No Strings' and tapping defiance to Horton, and later reprising it, on sprinkled sand, as a lullaby to Ginger; 'Cheek to Cheek', a dancing song-duet, with fantastic leaps and swirling, athletic grace; and, of course, the famous title song. As usual, much of the thunder was stolen by the exhilarating finale number, fast becoming a trade mark of the Astaire-Rogers films. There was the Carioca, then the Continental and now the Piccolino, staged at a fiesta at Venice

The song and dance saga

Lido and then danced in stylish ballroom fashion by Ginger and Fred, with the former singing the song at the beginning of the dance in wooing, caressing tones.

The 'Top Hat' number, by the way, was Fred's own idea. It came to him in bed one night when he was getting into rehearsal for a stage show called *Smiles,* He hit on a 'Young Man From Manhattan' sequence in which he tapped his cane and use it as a machine gun to bump off a 'gang' of chorus boys. As often happens the scene got lost in the show, but Fred later mentioned it to Irving Berlin who adapted the idea for *Top Hat.* One of the most nervous times Fred ever had, he says, was when Jimmy Cagney asked to visit the set of *Top Hat* and arrived just as they were shooting the machine gunning dance, which could have been a parody of Cagney's gangster films. All Jimmy said was: 'Use the second take, kid. That's far out the best.' When they came to see the rushes, Cagney was right.

The main problem of *Top Hat* was that the 'Cheek To Cheek' dance was nearly ruined. For once, Ginger's dress, a heavily feathered concoction, was not ready in time for the rehearsal. They usually had a few rehearsals in the clothes they were to wear in the dances during the actual shooting the next day. All kinds of snags can crop up when dancing with a partner in an ornamented gown instead of the shirt and pants Ginger usually wore for rehearsals.

This time, though, Astaire had to take it on trust. All hell broke loose when they started shooting, for Ginger's superb gown was covered with small white feathers which promptly started to moult as soon as the couple went into their dance. By the time they'd decided to risk it and ploughed through till the dance routine satisfied the director and cameraman the entire set looked as if a blizzard had set in.

For a very short time there was a distinctly cool atmosphere between the co-stars. But eventually, when everybody could see the ridiculous side of it, Hermes Pan and Fred concocted a parody—with apologies to Irving Berlin. It went:

'Feathers—I hate feathers,
And I hate them so that I can hardly speak.
And I never find the happiness I seek
With those chicken feathers dancing
Cheek to Cheek.'

Ginger could not resist the gag—or the gold brooch in the
form of a feather that accompanied it. All was forgiven and
Fred still occasionally calls her 'Feathers' affectionately, and
she still claims that *Top Hat* is her favourite of all her 70-odd
films.

While director Mark Sandrich was preparing the next of the
A. & R. series (as they were called in the studio), William Seiter
again took over the next Rogers film, *In Person*. In this one she
played a film star suffering from a bad attack of agoraphobia—
or 'the Garbos'. This passionate hatred of public places drove
her to the mountains, where she ran into George Brent. Brent
recognized her, but was standing no nonsense from her temperament and pretended that he didn't know her from Eve. With
her ego slightly bruised everything was set for some mild
complications and romancing before Brent cured her of her
phobia. Not a bad theme for a light comedy but still feather-
weight and distinctly unmemorable. Fortunately three more
musicals were to follow to keep the Rogers stock above par.

The first one found Ginger and Fred back in the safe, knowing
hands of Mark Sandrich in a breezy navy comedy called
Follow The Fleet; a change, if nothing else, because it enabled
Fred to doff his white tie and tails. He often wryly complained
that some people were convinced that he must have been born
in a top hat and tails; actually he has always been happier in
leisure clothes, and the hobo's clobber he wore in *Finian's
Rainbow*—slouch hat, kerchief, baggy pants—suited him down
to the last missing button.

Sandrich lined up a bright cast, though for once it seemed
that something vital was missing. Quite right: missing were

Eric Blore, Erik Rhodes and Edward Everett Horton, or equivalent eccentric characters. But there was their old sparring partner from *Roberta*, Randolph Scott—once more away from his Wild West horse co-stars—together with Harriet Hilliard, Lucille Ball, Betty Grable and handsome Tony Martin.

Astaire and Scott played a couple of jaunty sailors, with Fred as a hoofer who joined the navy when his dancing partner (Ginger) gave the heave-ho to his marriage proposal. Still, they met up later in time to win a dance contest. Meanwhile, Ginger and her sister were planning to turn a leaky old ship into a swagger showboat. So they staged a cabaret on board to wipe off the debt (cue for song-and-dance!). 'Easygoing yarn,' Fred once said to a reporter, 'but more than enough to give Ginger and me the chance to dance, and also for the cast to put over Irving Berlin's songs.' Little more was needed in an Astaire-Rogers musical.

Berlin, probably the most consistently successful Tin Pan Alley tunesmith over a lengthy period, surpassed himself yet again. Ginger and Fred had an exuberant duet, 'I'm Putting All My Eggs In One Basket', in the course of which the two frenziedly tried to outstep, knock into and gag with each other. It was splendid light hearted nonsense.

There were also such songs and routines as 'I'd Rather Lead A Band', 'Let Yourself Go' and a full-blooded chorus song by the gobs called 'We Saw The Sea'. As usual, the film went all out on a memorable finale. This time Berlin came up with 'Let's Face The Music And Dance', a superb ballet in which the educated feet of Fred and Ginger synchronized as never before. Or maybe it just seemed that way; the two appeared to blend more and more as one unit each time they danced. The final dance scena was exuberant, agile and romantic.

Follow The Fleet caused another dress incident—and once again Astaire was the fall guy. He examined Ginger's dress before rehearsals and thought it would be all right, though it seemed somewhat heavy because it was encrusted all over with beads. But he hadn't bargained for the heavy, hanging, beady sleeves. Whenever Ginger swung around Fred had to be on the alert to avoid being walloped by them. In the first take of the four-minute sequence Fred didn't weave in time and he did the rest of the take virtually unconscious. They took all day on the shot. Next morning, still exhausted from the gruelling dancing, they crawled into the studio to look over the rushes. The first take was the best—and the one that Sandrich used!

The studio could smell that *Follow The Fleet* was going to be another winner, and the critics were enthusiastic. *The Times* admitted that it was 'stereotyped', but insisted that it had 'some brilliant moments'. The *Observer* critic remarked pertinently that 'Ginger no longer dances as if she is afraid that she can't tap as fast as her partner'.

The success of *Follow The Fleet* meant that two decisions had to be shelved, temporarily at least. The studio magnates and the dancing magnets were wondering just how long they could press their luck and woo the public with their glittering but formula musicals. So far everything was fine. How long, though, before the public would decide that they'd seen enough? The public is the final prosecutor or defender.

Also Ginger for some time had had an urge to return to straight acting. She felt perhaps that with her new RKO star stature she would persuade the studio to let her play more serious roles than the fluffy, inconsequential ones that she had conscientiously appeared in since she arrived in Hollywood. She has said more than once that 'Great acting's not my line,' but she figured that she deserved a chance of playing some roles more meaty than 'leading man's girl friend'.

At this time she dearly wanted to play the role of Queen Elizabeth of England in a film Katharine Hepburn was scheduled to make for John Ford and took to disguising herself by making up as Elizabeth and then ensuring she was noticed by studio high-ups and directors. She even did an 'anonymous' test. But as soon as they realized that it was Ginger they'd grin and shake

(*above*) Clowning it up in *Red Peppers* by Noël Coward, Ginger's first big American television show (*below*) As chorus girl Fluff in *Young Man of Manhattan*, her first film (1930), with Charles Ruggles and Norman Foster

(*above*) Her first appearance with Fred Astaire, in *Flying Down to Rio* (1933) (*below*) Their last appearance together, 16 years later, in *The Barkleys of Broadway*

Ginger and Fred in *The Gay Divorce* (1934) It was the film that sent them on their light-footed way to stardom

Fred and Ginger take to skates for one of the numbers in
Shall We Dance? (1937)

their heads. This was their song-and-dance comedy girl. Ginger's frustration was intense.

But you can't interfere with a winning streak and arrangements were in hand for yet another Fred-Gin 'marriage'. They plunged into their sixth film together, *Swing Time*, with a fresh director, George Stevens, who was later to make many memorable films, notably *A Place In The Sun*, *Giant* and the great *Shane*, and with a score by the tip-top tunesmith, Jerome Kern. In the cast, Eric Blore and Helen Broderick were back from past hits and there was also the round-faced character actor, Victor Moore.

Frankly, I can't remember much about the story of *Swing Time* (if indeed it had one), but I do recall that it revolved round a dance band and that Eric Blore was as blandly comical as ever as the proprietor of a dancing academy. But though the limp, empty plot has passed into limbo the Kern numbers and the work of the hero and heroine are still vivid.

There was a long, jazzy vehicle for Astaire called 'Bojangles of Harlem', which involved a lot of trick process work and a chorus and didn't quite come off. But the other five dance-songs were well up to standard, blending gaiety, tenderness and knowing, sophisticated fun.

'Pick Yourself Up', danced on the bare floors of a practice room, became more than just a dance. It became almost an athletic event, and without a musical background. Then I remember Ginger radiant in a white gown, in contrast to Astaire's inevitable, impeccable dress-clothes, dancing the Swing-time Waltz; the cheeky lyric and bubbly tune of 'A Fine Romance', which the pair danced and sang with such humour against a snow scene; and Fred romancing Ginger with the love ballad 'The Way You Look Tonight', which won an Oscar.

As so often, though, it is the final song and dance sequence which remains in my memory since I first saw *Swing Time* years ago. 'Never Gonna Dance' was another of those songs which became a conversation-piece between Ginger and Fred. I recall his eloquent hands and wry smile luring Ginger into the dance, first slowly and hesitantly but building up to a final bursting excitement and then ending on a quietly wistful note of parting. It was light, immaculate dancing at its purest and most impeccable.

The film was followed by *Shall We Dance?* and this it seemed might well be the last of the cycle, for *Swing Time*, though liked by critics and audiences, did not do so well at the box-office after a brisk start. It was still a money-spinner, but the first signs of a decline were noticeable—and noted at the studio.

Though Nathaniel Shilkret was to direct *Shall We Dance?* the Pandro Berman-Mark Sandrich trademark was indelibly stamped on it. They came up with yet another bonus for their favourite musical stars; songs by George and Ira Gerswhin. There had to be nothing but the best for Ginger and Fred and the Gershwins were just right for this yarn about Fred as a ballet star who fell like a plummet for Ginger, a delicious swing dancer, and how Jerome Cowan, playing Ginger's manager, cut through the complications and got them together.

One of the film's top songs was 'Let's Call The Whole Thing Off', which was set in a park where Fred and Ginger, both wearing dark glasses to avoid recognition, made a date to row and skate. The song's charm and delight were clear to see and hear, but then the couple gave it a twist by turning it into a dance on roller skates. That was doing things the hard way, and Douglas McVay in his book on *The Musical Film* was among those who thought it unnecessary and that it didn't come off. I am inclined to agree that their agile footwork was bogged down somewhat by those skates.

But tolerantly, I think of the headaches of trying to dream up fresh, vivid ideas for a cycle of musical films which had set new standards for vitality, invention and surprise. Any wisp of an idea within the boundless dancing talents of Fred and Ginger must have been clutched eagerly and put to work.

No one could bicker at most of the other material: the brilliantly polished dance, 'They All Laughed', after Ginger had sung it as a solo; the opening 'Slap That Bass', which Fred sang and danced against the syncopation of ship's machinery; 'They Can't Take That Away From Me' and, of course, the finale, based on the title song.

The film had other joys too, notably an amusing scene with dogs being taken for their morning constitutional and Fred's funny take-off of a Russian choreographer. With stalwarts like Eric Blore and Edward Everett Horton again on hand, and the beautiful ballet star, Harriet Hoctor, to add to the decoration, *Shall We Dance?* was bound to prove popular.

But it started to dip at the box-office slightly earlier, even, than *Swing Time*. The series was clearly due for a rest. Astaire went into *A Damsel in Distress* with Joan Fontaine; Ginger was cast in one of her best straight parts in a comedy-drama called *Stage Door*.

Ginger and Lew Ayres had been dickering for quite a while as to whether they should try to solve their matrimonial problems by separation. 'We are still in love,' she told her friends, 'but living together is proving difficult.' It could be that Ginger's advancing film status was one of the problems, for Ayres was making no perceptible professional progress and, while he had his telescopes, appeared not to worry overmuch.

Anyway, they split. It was to be three years before they finally divorced, and they remained good friends. But there seemed no hope of patching up the incompatible association. Ginger bought a new house at the top of Coldwater Canyon where she still lives—it was the first of her many wise investments—and settled down to work.

Stage Door turned out to be one of the most entertaining comedy-dramas of the year and it had significance for Ginger. She made a decision that, as from *Stage Door*, she would 'have a go' at any reasonable role offered to her, no matter how different from anything she had tackled before. The film was one that played on characters' interreactions, dealing with the aspirations and mercurial fortunes of a group of stage hopefuls living in close, often jangling proximity in a theatrical boarding house.

Director Gregory La Cava had assembled a very useful cast. Apart from Ginger there were Katharine Hepburn, Constance Collier, Adolphe Menjou, Ann Miller, Jack Carson, Lucille Ball, Ralph Forbes, Gail Patrick and the dry, wisecracking Eve Arden. They all had a fair crack of the whip, with crisp dialogue and crucial scenes, and the result was a realistic picture which, as well as any that had ever been made, pointed to the uncertainties, heartbreaks, disappointments and ephemeral triumphs of theatrical life. Audiences enjoyed the vicarious kick they invariably get in watching other people struggling to overcome difficulties and troubles and the film proved a big success.

It was not easy to stand out in such company, for by then Oscar winner Katharine Hepburn, who played a society girl with stage ambitions, had proved in half a dozen films that she was on a short list of the screen's most fascinating young actresses; and a newish actress, Andrea Leeds, was quite superb. Still, the *Spectator*'s film critic stressed 'the brilliant, amusing rivalry between Rogers and Hepburn' and went so far as to write: 'Ginger Rogers acts Katharine Hepburn off the screen. Her talent is as certain as the parade-ground accuracy of her twinkling feet.' And of Ginger's performance as a flippant actress covering up her intense fear of failure *The National Board of Review Magazine* wrote: 'She's more than the lucky team mate of Astaire but a brilliant individual comedienne.'

The less said about *Having Wonderful Time*, in which Ginger was a city worker who went to a mountain camp for a holiday and fell in love with Douglas Fairbanks Jr., the better. It was a mild, ingenuous little comedy in which all the Jewish jokes and atmosphere which helped the stage version had been taken out. Its only minor point of interest was that it marked the film début of Red Skelton.

The song and dance saga

She followed this with a pleasant if uneven comedy with likeable, gangling James Stewart, *Vivacious Lady*. She played a glittering, razzle-dazzle night club singer who met and wed a shy young botany professor when he visited New York. The embarrassment started when he took his bride home to meet his small-town parents—a typical James Stewart situation. Stewart and Ginger made an amusing, relaxed team and Ginger sang a cute song called 'You'll Be Reminded Of Me', but audiences were again beginning to call for the joy of Astaire and Rogers musicals and shortly *Carefree* was ready to start shooting.

The filming of *Carefree* didn't mean that they and the studio had abandoned their idea of dissolving the partnership. Hanging on to a fading gimmick can be fatal. But the two stars were still such popular figures that it was merely a calculated risk on the part of the studio (and, thought many people, not even *much* of a risk) to give the musicals a final whirl or two before shutting up the shop.

Mark Sandrich, the director who probably had the shrewdest insight into the inimitable Astaire-Rogers technique, was to steer the film and the angle was to be a spoof on psychiatry. Fred was the psychiatrist who tried to use his skill to arrange a marriage between his lawyer friend Ralph Bellamy and radio singer Ginger Rogers. Naturally, Ginger soon fell for Fred instead.

This was the film which reaped a lot of advance publicity in papers and magazines with the momentous news that in *Carefree* Fred and Ginger would kiss. Even though the whole world was teetering on the verge of disaster this matter seemed to fascinate the masses as much as when Metro issued its staggering bulletin: 'Garbo Talks'. It shows what a hold entertainment can have on the lives and thoughts of millions when such matters *do* matter to so many.

This osculatory event had arisen because Ginger and Fred had never before kissed in their films. Someone worked up a rumour in the fan magazines that this was because Phyllis Astaire, Fred's wife, was jealous and refused to permit it. This suggestion, of course, was a load of nonsense, typical of some of the trash injected into fan mags for the sake of circulation. The fact was that the stars, and Pandro Berman and Mark Sandrich, had all agreed long before that it was a novelty not to have any truck with a lot of conventional romantic stuff in the films; that it was fresher and gayer for Fred and Ginger to do their wooing with their dancing rather than with the routine clinches.

It was decided that the 'kiss of the century' should be worked into the film. If they were going to break their rule they decided that they should do it with a flourish. 'Besides,' grinned Astaire, 'it will dispose of one international crisis.'

Among the four or five numbers written by that champion song-weaver Irving Berlin for the film was one called 'I Used To Be Colour Blind' which was to be a dream dance. The end was to be shot in slow motion and it seemed an apt slot for The Kiss.

Fred writes about it in his autobiography: 'When we shot the dance for slow motion it of course was danced in normal fashion. But the special camera for that sort of thing sizzles away at four times faster speed, so that when the film is run normally, the action moves four times slower.

'The dance finished with the celebrated kiss and we held that position in repose until the director called 'Cut'. Mark let it run on for a further 15 seconds to allow for a dissolve.'

Mrs. Astaire had been invited to see the rushes. The dance in slow motion looked graceful. Then, on the screen, came The Kiss. Fred and Ginger settled down, their lips frozen, as only a slow motion camera can suggest. The kiss held on the screen for four minutes. Director Mark Sandrich had deliberately rolled the camera extra time to put on this joke for Phyllis Astaire. When the film was shown it effectively knocked any suggestion that she was perturbed about her husband kissing Ginger on the screen.

The song and dance saga

The slow motion dance gave audiences a rare opportunity to examine closely the miraculous smoothness and dexterity of the couple's movements; the steps designed perfectly and with a machine-like symmetry and executed with such precision as to make it even more astounding that their dancing should so often suggest a relaxed, casual, improvised approach. Far from it. The seeming spontaneity came from hours of intense planning and rehearsal and the two experts had the confidence of people knowing what they were doing to the very flick of a toe.

Apart from the lushly designed, graceful 'Colour Blind', Berlin provided Fred with a Scottish lilt for a dancing routine in which he combined tapping with driving golf balls, and also an 'hypnotic dance' called 'Change Partners', which fitted neatly into the psychiatrist angle.

In his book, *Steps In Time*, Fred mentions how great Ginger was in this dance. But I fancy that he might have put it a shade more gracefully than when he wrote: 'Gin was swell, dancing as if in a trance the whole way through'. It is well-meant remarks like that which provide fodder for the acid-penned wisecracking critic in search of a gag at someone else's expense.

Carefree also introduced the Yam, a dance which was wonderfully exciting to watch, though it was not designed to become a ballroom favourite like the Carioca or even the Continental. But the Yam is almost an anthology of the Astaire-Rogers technique, with dash, movement, pauses, timing, élan and dramatic lifts; at the end it was gaily sung by the pair.

There was rather more slapstick and vigorous, happy-go-lucky comedy than in some of the previous films and Ginger revelled in the comedy, radiating mischief and the joy of life. She was hypnotized and put under anaesthetic and both scenes produced laughter; and, as critic Douglas McVay reminds us (and who *needs* reminding?): 'She is very sensuous and sexy in a delectably deadpan manner.'

Carefree was liked, but it didn't quite make the financial success that the studio by now automatically looked for from this great couple. It was decided that the party was over, and an announcement was officially made that the next film, to be started almost immediately, would be the wind-up.

The news did not go down all that well. For some people the musicals had become almost a way of life. There were letters of violent protest. Even some newspapers and show-business writers editorialized sadly about the break-up; it was not only the fans who were concerned.

Curiously, in what was planned to be their last film together, they were booked to make their first film in period costume. It had been decided to pay a screen tribute to a couple who, in a way, had been the predecessors of Ginger and Fred, and were certainly the pioneers of modern ballroom dancing.

The film was to tell *The Story of Vernon and Irene Castle*, and they were saddled with no easy task. Doing a film biography is always full of pitfalls, especially when the subject is still alive. Many of the problems were smoothed out, though, by the fact that Irene Castle worked closely on the film as adviser. She had already told Astaire that he was her choice to play Vernon Castle should their story ever be made into a film and, of course, Ginger was a natural choice as his partner.

Fred had known them well and seen many of their stage shows, so he was particularly and perceptively aware of their style. The producers were faced with a sticky problem. There could be no chance of bringing novel and characteristic Astaire-Rogers routines into the film; basically, they would have to concentrate on some of the numbers and dance routines that the Castles had created or made famous. There was plenty of first class material, but it was a barrier to Fred's invention.

For a long time the Castle Influence swept the world, changing the face of ballroom dancing and women's fashions and making impact on hair styles, house furnishing, social habits and so on. Both show business and society fell under the spell of this handsome, talented pair of image-formers. There would be a large number of people watching the film with ultra-critical, eagle eyes who 'knew the Castles when', or were prepared to believe they did.

But director H. C. Potter was unflappable. All he wanted was that a faithful tribute to the Castles should emerge, but without losing the vital personalities of Fred and Ginger. He built up a strong cast, including Edna May Oliver, Walter Brennan and Janet Beecher. It was a pity, in a way, that this would be the last of the series of musicals. It would have been a farewell treat to have had a final Fred and Ginger frolic in which, logically, typical roles could have been found for such old favourites as Erik Rhodes, Eric Blore, Jack Carson, Lucille Ball, Helen Broderick, Edward Everett Horton and the rest of the gang that had contributed their own individual stamp to the past pictures. That would have been an 'Auld Lang Syne' to cherish.

There's no doubt it was a song and dance fiesta. There were 14 song scenas and bits of 67 numbers were woven into the score, including such famous old favourites as 'Darktown Strutters Ball', 'Robert E. Lee', 'When You Wore a Tulip' and 'Pretty Baby'. The film also put over magnificently 'The Yama Yama Man' which was made famous by blues singer Bessie McCoy, and there was one particularly effective moment for Ginger when she danced to Fred as he sang a new song called 'Only When You're In My Arms'.

The film turned out to be very different and not really typical of the series, and its box-office takings underlined the wisdom of making the split. Still, both audiences and critics liked the film with reservations, and it was certainly a swan song of which Astaire and Rogers could reasonably be proud and which did justice to the memory of the dancing Castles.

I particularly remember the sure, confident manner in which Ginger handled the final difficult and touching scene after the death of the dashing Vernon Castle on military service. That alone dispelled any qualms anyone might have had that, as an actress, Ginger was a lightweight. When the material demanded she could rise strongly to the occasion.

The Castles met by accident while trying to fish a drowning dog out of a river. He manouevred to take her on a car trip. He proposed. Cue for two or three lively songs. Then, wed, they hit a roughish period until a break in cabaret enabled them to introduce their famous 'Castle Walk'.

From then on it was fame, fortune and international acclaim, and in skilful, fast-moving montage we saw them floating on winged feet through the capitals of the world. They became darlings of their age—the pre-World War I era—as they brought colour, panache and vivacity to night clubs and theatres with their fascinating foxtrots, tantalizing tangos, waltzes, one-steps and scintillating speciality dances. Soon Irene Castle had only to cut her hair short and every flapper was clamouring at her hairdresser for the Castle Bob. She influenced fashion vitally and Ginger must have had a ball selecting the rich, uniquely distinctive clothes she wore for the film.

The press in America and Britain were appreciative. The critics wrote of a 'worthy swan song' with a touch of nostalgic regret, but obviously realizing that Ginger and Fred were bowing out as a team at the right time. The inevitable menace of World War II was on the world's doorstep. Who could tell what would happen or whether the gaily irresponsible never-never world of the Astaire-Rogers musicals would soon be just an anachronism?

Ginger followed this film almost immediately with a straight comedy. While Astaire started a long list of musicals in which he seemed to partner every dancing star lovely in Hollywood (was he searching for a 'new' Ginger?) the determined Miss Rogers was convinced that the amicable split with Fred was the obvious opportunity to build up what she wanted—straight roles, both comedy and drama. She picked *Bachelor Mother*, for by now, of course, she was in a position to have quite a decisive say in what pictures she made. It was a sound choice. She was to co-star with David Niven, who was busily making films while pulling strings incessantly to get back to Britain and join up.

This he managed fairly quickly and did an excellent job—and *not* as a Whitehall Warrior.

Bachelor Mother, directed by Garson Kanin, who was later to make some outstanding comedies, notably *Born Yesterday*, sparkled throughout, with salesgirl Ginger fired from a department store by David Niven, the son of the owner. On the day she was fired she found herself 'adopting' an abandoned baby, which everybody thought was hers. The whole gang, including David Niven, fell over backwards to help her and, of course, romance flowered. But it was the crisp pace and bright dialogue rather than the thin story that helped this screwball comedy to be one of the brightest of the year. And Ginger was able to flash those exciting legs once more in a brief Charleston with Fred Albertson.

She was less lucky with *Fifth Avenue Girl* in which, as an un-employed girl, she was hired by a lonely millionaire to pose as his mistress so as to jerk his blasé family into noticing his presence. Director Gregory La Cava had hired some good solid actors—Charles Coburn, Franklyn Pangborn, Louis Calhern, —but no youngish male co-star. It is clear that Ginger, good-looker as she is, needed to be sparked off by a handsome guy and some romancing. Without one this film hardly got off the ground, though it tried to be a witty comment on the 'pity the poor rich' theme.

Chapter 6

GINGER TAKES STOCK

Britain—and much of Europe—was at war, but it was to be some time before the States moved into the bitter struggle for free existence. They had problems of their own. Superficially, the pattern of everyday life for Americans did not appear to change very much at the time, especially in the hard-working but lotus-like atmosphere of California. Nevertheless, many thinking Americans felt a sense of almost inevitable doom.

In her white haven at the crest of Coldwater, Ginger began to take stock. The war years were the beginning of a new era for the world; the end of the remarkably successful Astaire-Rogers musical series was the end of a personal professional era.

In roughly eight industrious years since she had arrived in the film capital from Broadway she had made 37 films, a huge output, and had become established as a Hollywood name. Apart from the nine pictures in which she had starred opposite Fred Astaire and which had made them world stars, how did the others rate?

Some were simply trashy potboilers turned out hurriedly and in slapdash fashion to keep the cinema wheels turning. A large number were not at all bad, serving their purpose of entertaining a large mass of folk who enjoyed relaxing, laughing, dreaming and being thrilled at the cinema and didn't want to think over-much or be badgered by sermons or messages, on the grounds that, at home or at work, they received enough mental and physical badgering. There is nothing wrong with such films provided they are made without pretension of high art and as professionally as time, the budget and talent allow. Some—films like *Stage Door*, *Bachelor Mother*, *Gold Diggers of 1933*, *Forty Second Street* and *Star of Midnight*—could be rated as good movies by most standards.

But, in her stocktaking, Ginger would have done herself injustice if she had genuinely blamed any of the flops and the 'not-so-hots' on her own performances. In eight years she had developed into a hard-working, conscientious and knowledge-able screen 'pro', capable of shining in any company, given a reasonable role and intelligent direction.

She was popular in Hollywood because she kept her nose clean. She was approachable to the press but never sought them out to curry publicity favours from them. She had not been lured into the café circuit around town simply because she was a keep-fit fanatic and the gadding around did not suit or amuse her.

She was beginning to take a keen interest in her financial future, and was sensible enough to know that financial security in the City of Dreams was the only stable asset. Press cuttings, the applause of audiences, the acclaim of critics, world fame, were of no value if the crunch came and your pulling power waned. Press cutting books have never yet been known to pay an outstanding bill. Ginger ignored the Hollywood attitude of so many stars in the halcyon days, stars who lived and spent as if there was not even going to be that evening, let alone a tomorrow.

She looked around her Coldwater Canyon house and knew that to purchase it had been a wise move Not long before, when things were more shaky financially, she had been living at the Garden of Allah Hotel with her mother. They were paying only $40 a week but Mrs. Rogers had wanted to pull out. Ginger had resisted. 'We'll hang on as long as we possibly can—people must not know that we're not doing too well."

Now, with the house bought for her mother, they were safe.

There were to be other investments including Rogers Rogue Ranch in Oregon (which was not to be simply a showplace but had to pay for itself). In five or six years' time she was to be officially listed by the Treasury in Washington as one of the ten biggest salary earners in the States, and much of the money would be wisely invested in oil and property so that Ginger need never work again unless she wanted to; more important, she need never do any work that didn't match up to her own standards. But as she took stock she did not know for sure that it would all work out this way.

Yet the girl from Independence, Missouri, was getting towards Independence fast and could be well satisfied with her first eight years in the jungle.

There was only one blot—the failure of her marriage to Lew Ayres. She told a friend: 'We thought we'd be together for ever. I can't tell at present whether we'll divorce. We're now just pals and often chat over the phone. I'm not embittered.'

But she was hurt and sad, for Ginger, though she has admitted that she seems to be a bad picker of men, is born for love and marriage—and with her the two cannot, ideally, be separated. Probably, when taking stock, she knew in her heart that she was crying in the wind when she said that she did not know whether she and Lew would be divorced. It seemed that it must happen. It was one battle scar in her early Hollywood campaign.

Now she closed the stocktaking and turned her eyes again to the studios. She was still ambitious, and there were interesting prospects awaiting her.

Chapter 7

AN OSCAR FOR KITTY

It is as well, maybe, that none of us has a reliable crystal ball in which to gaze with wistful, acquisitive or optimistic eyes. The knowledge that it is going to be a great year for one could be pleasant; to know that round the corner is a little man with a chopper just waiting to do us dirt and axe our dreams and hopes is a different cup of cyanide. Ginger was not to know that for her it would mostly seem like Christmas Day throughout 1940.

It started with a film called *Primrose Path*, with Ginger able to flex her muscles in a strong acting part. For the first time the girl who had lit up many a pleasant, if corny, film was involved in a seamy story on the screen. Not too seamy, of course, but enough to raise a few eyebrows.

With Gregory La Cava again in the saddle, Ginger played a down-to-earth 17-year-old, born on the wrong side of the tracks, who married an upright, promising young man. It wasn't the real thing—love—but Ginger married him from determination to escape from her evil mother, played insidiously by Marjorie Rambeau, and a fair old besom of a grandmother, for which Queenie Vasser was cast.

Of course, Ginger learned a lot about love and life through her young husband, very decently and stalwartly played by Joel McCrea. It was sheer soap-opera, but it gave Ginger a chance to get her teeth into a meaty role with some character and very different from some of the bubble-and-squeak she had

95

had to put up with during her apprenticeship. In fact, many people were hinting that Ginger was liable to find herself clutching a trophy on Oscar night for her striking performance as the kid who had it rough in *Primrose Path*. The tipsters were wrong as it turned out; but they simply chose the wrong film.

She went from this success to something of a filler in *Lucky Partners*. This was a comedy directed by Lewis Milestone, who had put Lew Ayres at the top of the heap with the film of *All Quiet*. But for Ginger the Milestone alchemy did not work in this piece about an artist who shared a sweepstake ticket with a girl who brought him luck. He then took her on an imaginary honeymoon to the moon, to the ire of her boy friend, Jack Carson, and it was an eminently forgettable piece of risqué nonsense with a few bright moments. Still, Ginger added Ronald Colman to the rapidly expanding list of top male stars with whom she had co-starred; that must have been some consolation.

Meanwhile, her next vehicle was being pondered. While she was filming with Colman a producer named David Hempstead handed her a copy of a book by Christopher Morley called *Kitty Foyle*. She was tired after making a couple of films. At first she tossed the book aside without even looking at it. Then one evening she did get around to it, but she was still mentally fagged out and really in no state to absorb the contents.

'I knew it was a colourful, adult role—the sort of thing for which I was constantly looking to shake off this image of a girl who had danced her way to success–but I didn't think it was for me. I called up the producer and said "I don't want to do it",' admits Ginger. That could have been that, just a mistake that she might live to regret. After all, years afterwards one producer abashedly admitted that he had turned down *Gone With the Wind;* there was that casting director who scrawled across the test card for Fred Astaire: 'Not film material. Dances a little—but can't act'; and still successfully working

An Oscar for Kitty

in London's Tin Pan Alley is a man who turned down the Beatles!

It can happen to us all.

So Ginger decided that she did not want to do *Kitty Foyle*. Instead of blowing his top the producer played it as cool as a slice of watermelon, and told her to go on a holiday, keep quiet, rest and have another look at it later. When she got back he sent the script round again and, refreshed mentally, she started to reread it. Everything fell into place; she laughed, she cried and she considered it one of the finest roles she was ever likely to have. She reached for the phone to call David Hempstead. Yes, this was the film she wanted.

Under Sam Wood's direction the filming started. The story was of a poorish salesgirl who fell hook, line and sinker for a rich society man from Philadelphia—it was Dennis Morgan's first big break—but found her real happiness with a man from her own class, James Craig.

There was nothing sensational about the role, but it had all the necessary ingredients, heart, sincerity and romance, plus the good old emotional tug-of-war between the rich and the poor. Ginger played it with warmth, intelligence and, above all, sympathy. When the film came out, those who had tipped her for a *Primrose Path* Oscar were in two minds. They thought that *Kitty Foyle* had an edge on the previous film. What did seem certain was that in 1940 Ginger would get her first Academy Award nomination. She did. In fact, she got the Oscar for *Kitty Foyle*.

A lot has been written and talked about the Oscar, much of it critical. But with all the hints, quite unfounded, of the voting being rigged, and the accusations of lobbying among studios and awards being handed out for sentimental reasons rather than for real acting prowess (which have rather more foundation), the Oscar remains the actor's accolade and Oscar Awards Night the fabulous, glittering showcase of the cinema industry.

GINGER—Salute to a Star

Ginger had won her award, ironically, for the type of role in which she was not yet fully accepted by her audience. Neither she nor Fred came within a whisker of winning one for all the delight they had given the world with their sparkling musicals. It is the way the movie dice fall. Remember that such cinema stalwarts as Cary Grant, Bob Hope, Charlie Chaplin, the late Judy Garland (bless her!), John Wayne, Shirley MacLaine and, incredibly, Greta Garbo never won the Thespian's Trinket.

Ginger had to beat off some tough competition. Arrayed in nomination beside her were Bette Davis for *The Letter*, Joan Fontaine, who starred in the eerie *Rebecca*, Martha Scott for *Our Town* and Katharine Hepburn for the sparkling *Philadelphia Story*.

With an old friend, Jimmy Stewart, getting the actor's award for *The Philadelphia Story* it was an entrancing and memorable night for Ginger. Alfred Lunt and Lynn Fontanne presented the Oscar to the actress, who was so excited that she forgot to thank them, but instead rushed to the microphone to deliver her prepared speech. Anyone expecting some inspired message or polished oratory from the radiant Ginger at that moment was doomed to disappointment. Excitedly, she hugged her mother and came out with the staggering cliché: 'It's the happiest moment of my life!' I think Ginger probably meant it.

From the drama of *Kitty Foyle* and all its prestige trimmings, Ginger, now firmly one of the Hollywood élite, picked one of those comedies which, I have always maintained, suit her bubbly personality better than all the histrionics.

Tom, Dick and Harry (a most uninspiring title) turned out to be fresh, cute and charming and in a lighthearted way did the Rogers image a lot of good. Basically, the idea was of a telephone operator unable to chose between three different swains, and, in her dreams, she tried to figure out her future with each.

With Burgess Meredith, Alan Marshall and George Murphy as the three suitors of varying classes and financial backgrounds, there was a neat vein of comedy throughout, and director Garson Kanin added to the studio fun by not telling the cast who was to win Ginger in the end. She did not know herself and used to haunt him with suggestions and guesses. Later it was remade as a musical called *The Girl Most Likely*, with Jane Powell, Cliff Robertson, Keith Andes and Tommy Noonan, and again it was a pleasant success.

It was after this film that Ginger invested in Rogers Rogue Ranch in Oregon. Her three leading men in *Tom, Dick and Harry* had talked so much about trout fishing while filming that she insisted on having a trout stream at the ranch. The main reason I would like to be rich is to be able to make sudden, extravagant decisions like that. As someone once sagely remarked: 'Money may not buy happiness, but with it you can rent enough.'

Professionally, it was an easy year for the energetic Ginger, with only one film. But it was the year that she finally shed her second marriage, leaving Lew Ayres to his telescopes and a strange, introspective life which led him to become a sergeant in the army a couple of years late and eventually return as a passionate, avowed conscientious objector, which did not help his film career. Later he was to make occasional religious films.

When Ginger married Lew her career was rising and so was her popularity with the public. One newspaper assessed the number of proposals she received flooded in at around 3,000 a week. This was without doubt a stupid, reckless guess, but there is no doubt that her fan mail was large. Lew's career was not flourishing and his fan mail was correspondingly tailing off. In the tinsel business of stardom these pointers matter—and stir up a sullen resentment.

It was also printed and not, as far as I can find out, denied that the final break came when Lew suddenly said to Ginger: 'I wish you'd go home to your mother and stay there.' According to the report she went, and that ended this frayed romance.

Of his broken marriage Lew said nothing except, when the final decree was going through, to remark quietly: 'I never had time to see my wife.' This has been the sad epitaph of many dual-career marriages, especially in Hollywood's all-demanding atmosphere.

The break-up of the Ayres-Rogers marriage, though it had been so prolonged as almost to be forgotten, stirred up the gossip hounds again and Ginger's name was linked with George Murphy's, on the strength of a few friendly dates with the actor who was one of her leading men in *Tom, Dick and Harry*. One item even linked her with the French actor, Jean Gabin. Ginger shrugged. She had just come out of one long marriage tunnel and had no intention of popping into another.

Besides, the British reviews of the film were coming over and she found them good reading. C. A. Lejeune of the *Observer* described Ginger as 'going through the film as if in an enchanted dream'. William Whitebait in the *New Statesman* praised her, writing: 'Ginger . . . acting with abandon, behaving outrageously; being silly and charming, herself and a caricature of herself.' Ginger must have glowed when she read the knowledgeable and experienced Dilys Powell of the *Sunday Times*, who turned cartwheels when she wrote: 'Ginger Rogers surpasses her performances in *Kitty Foyle* and *Primrose Path*. She is pure enchantment as the small-town romancer and schemer . . . one day we'll be remembering Ginger as now we remember Mary Pickford and the Gish Sisters.' Heady praise to read quietly by a swimming pool in California. It was hinted in the papers that Ginger was contemplating a musical with George Murphy, but Ginger's eyes were set on drama.

Roxie Hart gave Ginger a startling change of character and not everybody enjoyed it. It took her back to some of her earlier, flip chorine roles, but this time the character was tougher, more brazen and amoral. It was based on a play called *Chicago*, and William Wellman directed a Nunnally Johnson story that pulled no punches in its brittle comedy.

An Oscar for Kitty

She played a wisecracking, publicity-mad floozy of a chorus girl who, to get her name on the front pages in a newspaper fiesta, took the rap for a murder her husband had committed. There was no real risk for the girl. It was set in the lawless Chicago of 1927.

'They wouldn't even hang Lucrezia Borgia in those days,' gagged one character. Ginger pretended to be pregnant to get sympathy, and her fly, astute lawyer, played by Adolphe Menjou with a chilly, smiling smoothness, even arranged for the trial to start on Mother's Day.

Though the film was outrageous, cynical and often coarse, I thought it frequently very funny, with the edgy banter between Ginger, Menjou and the other characters. There was also the chance of seeing those rhythmic, well-shaped legs go into a dance for the first time since the very different Castles film. Watching her do a peppy Charleston and an equally zippy Black Bottom in a jailhouse tap rolled back the calendar a few years, and the *New Statesman* described it as the best light film for months.

Dilys Powell of the *Sunday Times* thought she overplayed the brazen little cutie, while Raymond Durgnat in his probing and often perceptive book *The Crazy Mirror* even detected sinister influences. He wrote: 'It shows the brutality of U.S. justice versus the U.S. sentimentality . . . each exposes the other as a parody of commonsense. It's both cynical and puritan.' So that is what this sharp-moving comedy, cunningly geared for laughs, was supposed to do?

After this minor furore she entered a very indifferent patch, with one or two exceptions. *Tales of Manhattan* was one of those portmanteau yarns with four or five star-crusted episodes all linked by one theme—in this case the vicissitudes of a dress suit. Hopefully the makers of such films gamble that one or two of the episodes, at least, will hit the mark. Ginger, with Henry Fonda and Cesar Romero, was left high and dry in the second and most feeble of the vignettes. R.I.P.

GINGER—Salute to a Star

Billy Wilder's *The Major And The Minor* followed, however, and restored the balance. This was a gay, wacky comedy which Steven H. Scheuer, in *Movies On TV*, has described as 'often risqué but never offensive'. In it Ginger disguised herself as a child to get home half-fare on the train and got tangled with an army major going to visit his fiancée. Ginger, of course, fell in love with him, with inevitable complications. Ray Milland played the man and Ginger gave a really fresh and delicious performance, proving once again that her sense of comedy could stand up to that of any woman on the screen. The scenes between the hapless Milland and the knowing young girl were charming. Ginger's mother, Lela, was roped in to play her screen mother and it all went well in every way.

At this stage in 1942 Hollywood was beginning to think that it should give some of its films a war angle, but by then America had not fully recovered from the vicious Japanese attack on Pearl Harbor. Producers had not had time to think, as had the British, how the cinema could best be used for propaganda pictures that would also entertain the masses. They started to flirt with the idea, though, by inserting war characters and themes into their ordinary films. At least it proved that they were aware that some seriousness had to be blended with the staple entertainment that was needed to keep up civilian morale. What could actresses like Ginger and her colleagues do but carry on with the jobs they knew best and try to keep up the spirits of their countrymen?

A valid point, which was as much a problem in Britain. But Hollywood's early attempts were feeble and could not have given much satisfaction to responsible citizens in the film world. Ginger, for example, was drafted into a moderate comedy with Cary Grant and Walter Slezak and directed by Leo McCarey. It was a satire which did not have enough edge. It fulfilled a purpose in providing some middling relaxation but its wartime theme had the air of being swiftly dreamed up to make it topical. Grant played a U.S. reporter; Ginger the wife of Slezak, a Gestapo agent. Cary trailed Ginger so as to be able to give first hand reports of Hitler's conquests but complicated matters by getting enamoured with her. The humorous twists never quite came to life.

At least that film, *Once Upon A Honeymoon*, was intended for laughs. *Tender Comrade*, which followed, with Robert Ryan, was a very sticky cup of goo, of which *The Times* wrote 'artificial ... even that intelligent actress, Ginger Rogers, is defeated'. She played a defence worker (get the war angle in, see?) whose husband was away fighting. She shared a house with several similar women and they spent their time bravely and patriotically carrying on and sentimentalizing over their courtships and marriages. It was a mass of goodbyes and being brave. Ugh!

Curiously, this unimportant offering got a lot of publicity in an unexpected way. It was written by Dalton Trumbo and directed by Edward Dmytryk, both confessed Communists. Ginger and her mother, politically alert and as all-American as cranberry pie, were horrified at some of the lines, denigrating United States democracy, which she was supposed to say in the film. She rebelled—and if she believes that she is in the right she has a mighty stubborn streak. Eventually she compromised, for the sake of the film, allowing the lines to be uttered by other actresses in the cast.

Tender Comrade was the only film Ginger made in 1943. She had found a more rewarding outlet, while sticking to the job she did so well. She made several ten-minute training films, including one with Walter Huston which was regularly used by the U.S. Services and called *Safeguarding Military Information*. With Spencer Tracy she narrated another military film and she also made a trailer called *Ginger Rogers Funds* to help the fourth War Loan Drive.

On paper this may not sound a terrific contribution, but it was constantly pointed out that stars were still needed at their own jobs to keep the giant film business healthy both financially and professionally, and anybody who ever found himself on leave or posted to an out-of-the-way dump of a town which didn't boast a cinema knew the value of pictures as pepper-uppers and dispellers of the blues. With so many stars disappearing into the forces the onus fell even more heavily on the feminine stars.

Ginger was soon to make another bid for her heart's desire—married happiness. She was touring with the United Services Organization, an activity she found very worth while. She was able to revert to song and dance, and her gaiety and friendliness must have been a bigger boost to the lads than an extra beer ration. Her starry name and film-star reputation all added to the kick, of course. She was meeting the men as well as the officers, collecting notes for home, delivering home-town messages. For a while she was a long way from the synthetic Hollywood goldfish bowl, and she felt like a youngster playing truant from school.

Then it happened—for the third time.

It was a troop show at a base at San Diego. It could have been the war atmosphere and its excitement; it could have been the uniform; it could have been that he was tall, good-looking and stalwart. Who knows? She met a Marine and within weeks—on January 6th, 1943—she was Mrs. Jack Briggs. She married her Marine in an empty Methodist church in Pasadena. There was no one around, no cameras were clicking, no fancy reception afterwards. The groom was in uniform and she wore a brown tailored suit. Did her memory slip back a few years to a very different wedding and to a reception at a swanky hotel when she and her husband, Lew Ayres, had ducked the guests, columnists and rubbernecks and gone off bowling?

This was a very different ceremony and, Ginger optimistically dreamed, a very different marriage. This was to be third time lucky and for the third time Ginger was convinced that it would be for ever. 'Jack is all I've every dreamed of,' she said.

An Oscar for Kitty

Ah well. . . .

They had a brief honeymoon and then it was back to the Marines for Jack and to the studios for Ginger. When he was demobilized he moved into the white house on the hill. But he was no longer Marine Jack Briggs. Now he was a small-time actor again and the husband of a big shining star. After his honeymoon he must have had some good-natured ribbing from his Marine pals, to whom Ginger was an unattainable screen goddess. Judging from his hefty frame, though, I doubt if anyone took the rash chance of chaffingly calling him 'Mister Rogers'.

When the honeymoon was over and 1944 was looming up, and with her husband away, it seemed high time for Ginger to get back to her craft. Though no longer under contract to RKO she was in a better position, a highly paid freelance and much in demand.

The trade papers insisted that at this time she was contemplating forming a $3,000,000 production company with producer Charles Koerner. Instead her first bosses, Paramount, wooed her again with a tempting picture. She was asked to play Liza Elliott in Moss Hart's *Lady In The Dark*, the Ira Gershwin-Kurt Weill musical which had starred Gertrude Lawrence on Broadway and which she had just finished touring. It was the stage musical in which Danny Kaye was first noted and which teed off his fabulous career. Later, an excerpt from it was reconstructed for the film *Star*, in which Julie Andrews loosely played the Gertrude Lawrence life story.

Ginger hadn't sung or danced seriously in films for some years. (We can forget her brief, lively jiving spots in *Roxie Hart*.) She was enjoying her life as a straight film actress. Yet the invitation was irresistible. Everything seemed to be going for *Lady In The Dark*. The part was fascinating, the numbers were smart, there was lush sparkle in the clothes and fun in the situations with Ginger playing a variety of ages. What probably decided Ginger was that it was to be her first all-colour film

—a distinct challenge. Ginger has never dodged a challenge.

The picture concerned a svelte fashion editress who was subject to frequent headaches and daydreaming. She was psychoanalysed to find the cause and, of course, there was plenty of scope for dream sequences, usually a natural for a lighthearted film. Yet, without being a failure, it turned out to be a disappointment. Why? It is difficult to pinpoint. It is the sort of question that has been haunting film-makers ever since John Bunny and Flora Finch were the prevailing stars.

It was not lack of talent. Apart from Ginger, who tackled the role with vivacity, there were such sound actors as Ray Milland, Warner Baxter and Mischa Auer. There were some sparkling songs, notably the haunting 'Jenny', 'My Ship' and the still-recalled 'Suddenly It's Spring'.

It was not that the film was made skimpily. The sets were lavish and so were Ginger's clothes. She wore a mink worth over $10,000, a wedding dress which set the studio back nearly $3,000 and a sequinned gown that cost even more. Ginger wore these trimmings with flair.

Moreover, colour suited Ginger. It brought out her fresh complexion and the tints of her auburn-blonde hair as black and white could never do. The film, however, presented problems. The heat of working under colour cameras was very trying. Ginger had to dance in high heels and a bouffant skirt. Above all, after several years of not dancing she had to rehearse for six hours a day for four weeks to perfect her footwork with Dan Loper. The finished film turned out to be a case of Lady In The Dim.

Nor did the next one do her proud. This was a sentimental trifle with Joseph Cotten and Shirley Temple directed by William Dieterle, called *I'll Be Seeing You*. Dieterle was not happy about it and told me much later: 'I tried to keep the sentiment down but the screenplay defeated me. The sentimental stuff kept oozing out like warm treacle. You couldn't blame the actors.' There was even a Christmas supper sequence with all the seasonal trimmings and the family singing 'O Come All Ye Faithful', but the best musical asset was the title song, written by Sammy Fain and Irving Kahal, which Frank Sinatra helped to make famous somewhat earlier.

Ginger was a convict on Christmas parole (said the *Manchester Guardian*: 'Such is her potent charm that it's strong enough to enable her to keep her shoulder length hair') who met Sergeant Joe Cotten, just discharged from a mental home after shell-shock. She invited him home to meet the folks, keeping mum that she was a jailbird until little sister (Shirley Temple) blurted it out. Nevertheless, love blossomed despite the complications. There was no need to worry overmuch about Ginger being in jail; be sure it was an accident. She was serving a manslaughter charge after accidentally killing her boss when he drunkenly attacked her. The *News Chronicle* thought it 'lachrymose' though *Time* was charitable enough to toss a nosegay to Miss Rogers' 'moments of warm sympathy'. But stretch the Christmas spirit to its utmost and you still could not regard this as anything but a sentimental potboiler.

Ginger had earlier faced a challenge which is always tough on an actor, that of standing up to comparison with previous stars. She had taken the risk when playing the role of Irene Castle and the one created by Gertrude Lawrence. Now the situation cropped up again and Ginger was not fazed by her task. She was signed to play in Metro's *Weekend at the Waldorf*, a remake of the star-laden *Grand Hotel*, which had Garbo, John Barrymore and a host of similar names.

The new version was to be equally starry. Guy Bolton had updated it from Vicki Baum's novel and the earlier screen version, and Metro had lined up such names as Ginger, Lana Turner, Van Johnson, Walter Pidgeon and Edward Arnold. Ginger was faced with the nervous task of playing in the footsteps of Garbo, the Great Swede. Of course, there are always some who look back in anger—or sentiment—and cannot resist making detrimental comparisons. Actors and actresses learn to live with it as a thorny occupational risk, but it can still be a worry.

In the first version Garbo played a mystery adventuress. Ginger's character in *Weekend at the Waldorf* was more clear-cut. She played a poised, successful film actress and Walter Pidgeon was a war correspondent. They shared what were, I think, the best scenes in a film deftly directed by Robert Z. Leonard. One night Pidgeon slipped into Ginger's room on an urgent mission —but it was not the obvious one! She mistook him for a thief but, with that intuition and goodness of heart characteristic of her sex, decided to give him shelter. There were those who thought that it would have been better if Ginger and Lana Turner (who played a demure typist who dreamed of Park Avenue but settled for the more homely Van Johnson) had exchanged roles, but my feeling was that the movie still worked out reasonably well. It was adult and elegant and offered some star performances.

Ginger also added to her reputation for being one of the best dressed women on the screen. In this one she wore 12 different gowns designed by Irene and with a different coiffeur for each. Hollywood never underrated the interest of women cinemagoers in the clothes they saw on the screen.

Another—not so bright—remake followed with *Heartbeat*, a rather trashy little exercise in which Ginger had again to bear comparison, this time with an attractive French predecessor, Danielle Darrieux. It was a dull, banal film—the first in which Ginger did not play an American or a Canadian—with the heroine as a destitute girl trained by Basil Rathbone to pick pockets. She fell in love with Jean Pierre Aumont, a handsome young diplomat whom she was supposed to rob; and Sam Wood, who directed it, seemed little in love with the subject and did not give his cast much inspiration to do more than jump through emotional hoops.

By now Ginger must have thought that she had more than

served her apprenticeship in routine pictures which did not even give her a glimmer of a chance to show that bubbly personality and comedy sense which had made her a prime favourite. She must have decided that she had little to lose by seeking and taking a chance on more serious roles. But when the screenplay of *Magnificent Doll* reached her she sensed a tricky task ahead. Yet Ginger was interested in playing in *Magnificent Doll*, largely because it would be her first chance to tackle a slice of American nineteenth-century history. A story about politics, too, in which Ginger was intelligently interested.

Politics? Nonsense. The producers at Universal were more interested in histrionics than in history. Ginger played Dolly, the wife of James Madison, a kindly, philosophical character who was America's fourth president. The plot revolved almost entirely around the notorious affair that Dolly Madison had with Aaron Burr, a traitorous character who had only two desires, (*a*) to possess Dolly and (*b*) to become Emperor of the Americas, and saw no reason why he shouldn't combine his ambitions. Burr was a thorough-paced heel, but he had a debonair charm which David Niven brought out admirably and it's little wonder that Dolly Madison fell for him, though still in love with her quiet, mild husband, played by Burgess Meredith.

Incidentally, David Niven's tiny son Davy Junior (now a high-powered young producer-executive in London) showed early signs of that instinctive character reading which is now standing him in good stead. He asked his father to tell him about this man Burr. David blunderingly tried to explain and the lad cut him short by saying: 'I see, he was almost as bad as Hitler, wasn't he?' 'Exactly,' replied the relieved father, 'but they caught up with Burr in time.'

The combined talents of Ginger, Niven, Meredith and Horace McNally, who played Ginger's first husband, made this an acceptable but not noteworthy film. Women, of course, revelled in Ginger's wardrobe, for the actress was proving herself not only a warm, popular screen personality but also what Hollywood described as 'one helluva fine clothes horse'. In other words, when a producer lashed out on extravagant, eye-filling gowns for Ginger he knew she could wear them in a way that would show up in the right place—on the screen. In this one she wore 25 different costumes of the period, all designed by one of Hollywood's top fashion experts, Banton, and she looked a dream.

Collectors of trivia may also care to know that *Magnificent Doll* probably set up a record which, as far as I am aware, has not since been beaten. Director Frank Borzage, after a quick glimpse through the final script, instructed his continuity girl, Adèle Cannon, to make a note of the number of kisses that Ginger had to enjoy (or endure) in the film. It fully made up for the lean osculatory years during the Astaire-Rogers era. Anyone who happens to be writing a thesis on the subject may care to know that with rehearsals, takes and retakes, Horace McNally, playing her first husband, kissed Ginger 62 times. Her president-husband, Burgess Meredith, managed 87 kisses; David Niven, playing the opportunistic, rascally Burr, came up with lip-service no less than 212 times.

If there is a moral to this story it is that the rogue in an eternal triangle usually comes off best. The other moral, of course, is that kissing may go by favour but that it doesn't necessarily follow that audiences will favour the film that has the kissing. Ginger's dabbling with politics on the screen was *not* a huge success.

It was in 1947—my first visit to Hollywood—that I first met and split an ice cream soda with Ginger. I remember that my main impression was of a thoroughly happy young woman doing a job she liked and doing it very well.

Financially she was sitting pretty. Astuteness on her part and that of her mother and her agent had steered her into a high money bracket, especially at a time when Uncle Sam was not clawing at income tax so sharply as nowadays. Enterprise Films had reportedly negotiated a deal which upped her bargaining power, as had an earlier one with David O. Selznick. Ginger, as a freelance, could now reportedly command something like $175,000 a picture plus a cut of the gross takings, which varied with the projects from 10 per cent to 40 per cent.

When I first visited the Coast she was making another romantic comedy, *It Had To Be You*, with Cornel Wilde and Ron Randell, at Columbia. I also met Randell for the first time then and he summed up Ginger as 'a very living doll'. The film was an able piece of froth and, curiously enough, not for the first time in Ginger's films dream sequences played an important part. She was a socialite who three times had stood up her groom at the altar and it was becoming something of a complex. The right man in the end turned out to be a fireman, played by Wilde.

Having seen bits of the film being made I was naturally even more interested than usual in the opinions of my British colleagues on the film. Stephen Watts of the *Sunday Express* went to town on Ginger, if not the film, writing: 'Somewhere in the archives of the late Lubitsch there must be a glorious comedy to exploit the gifts of that delightful female clown, Ginger Rogers. She skilfully tosses off a funny line to make it funnier or improves an already funny situation.' Fred Majdalany, in the *Daily Mail*, called her 'a fine comedienne who can keep alive a joke she has seen through'.

'The Matchless Ginger. Nobody ever snuggled up to a man more divinely,' said the *Daily Herald* man omnisciently. While Leonard Mosley of the *Daily Express* praised her performance, adding the sheepish rider: 'But then I've always adored Ginger. When I lived in Hollywood I used to track her down, unavailingly, at parties.' It must have been bewildering for Ginger, aspiring to series roles, to find how appreciated and cherished were her light comedy performances.

In *It Had To Be You* Ginger became a screen bride for the

thirteenth time; but her own matrimonial problems were not
going so blithely. Her marrige to ex-Marine Jack Briggs was
not working out. Several people in Hollywood told me so at the
time, not bitchily but regretfully. Some actresses will discuss
their private lives quite freely, but soured marriages are not
something that one can discuss with Ginger in depth unless one
has the hide of an armadillo. The marriage was apparently
drifting—again on those rocks of incompatibility; but Ginger
was not one to rush in and out of marriages and this one was
to drift on for another couple of years before the divorce.

She was very active at the time. There was talk in the
papers that she was to run for Congress as a representative for
California. I recall asking Republican Rogers about this and
about what would be her platform. She smiled gaily enough and
replied 'Cheaper and better ice cream for all', and that was
enough hint to me that the rumour was nonsense, for she is not
one to joke about matters that she takes seriously. Later, in the
press, it was all denied. Some hard-bitten but jaded columnist
had dreamed up the item to fill her column.

Lela Rogers, though, was very politically involved at the
time. She was called upon to testify before the Un-American
Activities Committee which was campaigning against Com-
munist infiltration. To suspect the 100-per-cent-American
Rogers family of disloyalty was, of course, ridiculous. Remember
that Ginger even insisted on having her lines rewritten in the
film *Tender Comrade* because some of them smacked of anti-
Americanism. I bet, though, that they were also not very good
lines.

Then, in 1949, came news that excited her fans.

People remembered the halcyon years of the *Top Hat* and
Carefree swinging films and had been hoping for another series.
The news was not to work out like that; there was just the
announcement of a one-film get-together.

Metro-Goldwyn-Mayer had signed Charles Walters to direct
a backstage musical film called *The Barkleys of Broadway*, with

An Oscar for Kitty

Fred Astaire and Judy Garland, but Judy, suffering one of those nervous illnesses which were to help to hasten her sad death, had to turn down the film. Leo the Lion was stuck until someone rather nervously suggested that they contacted Ginger. What was their worry? Well, it was ten years since Ginger and Fred had worked together and in that time Ginger had stuck with determination to her decision to break away from musicals and concentrate on comedies and, where possible, more serious films. Besides, someone distantly recalled, hadn't there been talk that the two didn't get on too well together?

Ginger scotched all the rumours by saying yes at once to the idea of taking over from Judy. 'I think it will turn out to be fun,' she told Chuck Walters and Fred. It was her usual attitude to a job that she wanted to do, and it *did* turn out so.

Curiously, the story had some resemblance to the careers of Fred and Ginger, except that in the film the Barkleys were married and a brashly temperamental pair of bickerers. But the theme was the clash when one of the two partners wanted to toss aside working in musicals and concentrate on heavier drama.

The plot and the uneven dialogue, however, much of which was not so witty as it must have seemed in the screenplay, were not allowed to obtrude too much on the singing and the hoofing which was what the customers were eager to see and hear. The musical side had some good stuff in it with songs from Ira Gershwin and Harry Warren and some that didn't quite come up to the standards set by the pair before the war.

But there was no question that time had done nothing to mar the perfect rapport between these two cultured performers. It was the first all-colour film they had made together and the colour suited them. They still danced together like a smooth dream; their timing and harmony and sense of 'being together' were as irresistible as a few years earlier. The return of Astaire and Rogers—which really *was* to be their swan song as a team —completely defeated the fast moving calendar.

Oscar Levant, the pianist-wit with the mordant, sarcastic delivery, provided most of the humour in the dialogue, together with a typically witty Billie Burke performance. Some of Ginger's lines were not quite right for her and she probably inherited them from the script designed for Judy. But among the musical numbers there were three or four well worth remembering.

Not, I think, 'My One And Only Highland Fling', in which Fred and Ginger were togged up in kilts and rather over-played the spoof Scottish accents. Too much mugging for my taste. This was originally, I suppose, intended for Fred and Judy Garland as a follow-up of their brilliant 'We're A Couple of Swells', but it did not come off. Strangely, in her Desert Island Discs programme Ginger included this as one of her choices. Maybe it was a sentimental gesture to mark her final film with Fred, but I doubt if even Ginger could bear to hear it too often even when marooned on an island with a limited record repertoire.

I remember, though, a slick, jazzy dancing duet reminiscent of 'I'm Putting All My Eggs In One Basket' which they put over in *Follow The Fleet*. This one harked back to many similar dancing duos and, I think, showed them at their best, relaxed, carefree and clearly having a good time. There was also another exhilarating high spot, a version of 'They Can't Take That Away From Me' played against a soft pink background. Of course, no Astaire-Rogers film would be complete without a finale to send audiences home with a feeling of *joie de vivre*. This one had Fred singing 'Manhattan Downbeat' to his partner and finally dancing to it with her on a packed, colour-ful stage, the whole screen alight with movement.

And so the curtain finally went down on the dancing supre-mos, Fred and Ginger, though both were to go on to other work, other big successes. But it was the well-timed end of the Magnificent Two. There's always a cue for exit music.

There was a scene where Ginger played the young Sarah

An Oscar for Kitty

Bernhardt and excited the Académie Française by reciting 'La
Marseillaise'. Critics should have been disarmed by Ginger's
frequent admissions that she has never regarded herself as
another Duse.

But when the film was shown lately on television the scene
called forth comment from the television critic of the *Sun*, who
wrote waspishly: 'If Ginger Rogers, in her Drury Lane dressing
room, caught this bit of *The Barkleys of Broadway*, did she laugh
or cover her eyes and groan: "Oh, my Gahd"?'

Ginger might equally ask, had she the opportunity, if the
ever facetious Miss Nancy Banks-Smith of the *Sun* has ever
looked back on her columns of ten years ago and laughed? Or
groaned, 'My Gahd!'

That year Ginger and Jack Briggs were divorced.

The man who was 'everything I have ever dreamed of' had
apparently turned out less than that. The divorce came under
the glib, irritating excuse of 'cruelty', so often dragged up in
American unhitchings. Very rarely is this unchivalrous
'cruelty' manifested in a positive way, such as giving the wife a
brace of beautiful shiners or dragging her, half naked, on to the
front lawn and thrashing her with a razor-strop in front of the
neighbours. At least, then, cruelty would be done and seen to be
done. Cruelty in American divorces usually means something
like eating fish and chips in bed and using your wife's navel to
hold the salt; or not allowing her to use the spare Oldsmobile to
date her boy friend, or similar trivialities.

Ginger certainly did not rush the divorce out of petulance.
In her plea of cruelty she insisted that her husband would
constantly leave the house without saying where he was going
or giving her any idea when he would be back; he would come
home at all hours, again without explanation; above all, he
developed an irritating habit of falling asleep in front of her
guests—even at the dinner table.

It seemed a clear case of incompatibility. The woman who,

somehow, could not pick a winner in the love stakes was free again.

So back to the studios.

Her journey to Warner's was hardly necessary. *Perfect Strangers* (shown in Britain under the title of *Too Dangerous to Love*, since the American title had already been used for a Robert Donat film) was a routine, contrived weepie in which she and Dennis Morgan, her partner in *Kitty Foyle*, fell in love while serving on a murder jury. But neither was free and after a good deal of hearts-and-flowers small talk they decided to go their separate ways. Unmourned, I must add, by the audiences.

But the same studio pulled an interesting film out of the bag for a follow-up. This was a harsh, steely melodrama about the Ku Klux Klan menace, called *Storm Warning*. The part was said to be intended originally for Lauren Bacall, but she had another commitment. Ginger eagerly accepted the film as a distinct change of pace from some of her recent comedies.

Ginger played a model who, visiting her young married sister (an early performance by Doris Day before she got swept up in musicals) in a Southern town, was witness to a murder by a gang of Ku Klux Klanners. But she lied when testifying in the box, for one of the men she had recognized as her brother-in-law. How could she send him to the chair?

After he drunkenly assaulted her, however, she lost her qualms. The Klan had to silence her; she was abducted and taken to one of their ritual meetings and mercilessly whipped. With Steve Cochran as the 'heavy' and Ronald Reagan (now elevated to high political rank), *Storm Warning* was an often tense drama which surprised many who still persisted in regarding Ginger merely as a gay, talented wisecracking song-and-dance star. Leonard Mosley of the *Daily Express* was impressed enough to write boldly: 'She earns the right to put actress after her name.'

Even Ginger's standing in the business did not make it a clear-cut certainty that she would get the type of picture for which she was constantly hoping. There was talk of her going into production for herself, but the various hints in the trade press petered out. Meanwhile, Ginger made a 'comedy' which just about touched rock bottom for dullness and stupidity. Universal lured her into *The Groom Wore Spurs* with Jack Carson. Ginger, no fool when it comes to assessing a script, must have been having a jaded spell when she agreed to appear in this uninspired nonsense, in which she played a lawyer hired to keep a dumb cluck of a high-living, cowboy film star out of trouble. The more jams he got into the more she fell for him, but when the film came out it was obvious that Ginger was the one who had got herself into a jam.

It stood out like amiable Jimmy Durante's famous schnozzle that a few more lame pictures such as this could harm even Ginger's reliable track record. She figured rightly that it was time to take stock again.

Chapter 8

FRENCH POLISH

'I'll have to sleep with it under my pillow for a few nights to see if it sticks in my ribs.' This was Ginger's quaint reply to playwright Louis Verneuil, when he asked her to consider starring in his new play *Love And Let Love*.

A return to the theatre after about 20 years of filming? This, she thought, could be the answer to her problem, for Ginger was wise enough to know that there *was* a problem. There was no question of her career tottering or offers for films drying up; both were solid. But she had been around Hollywood long enough to know that one more *Groom Wore Spurs* could lead to similar loads of rubbish if she were not wary.

A spell away from Hollywood and its synthetic atmosphere might well be a solution. She read and reread the play, in which she would be playing two roles, a flighty young woman and her demure, home-loving sister, and it began to 'stick in her ribs'. Playing the dual role was a challenge. The play gave her plenty of opportunity for wearing good and varied clothes (and Ginger knew very well that that is an important 'plus' for women theatregoers), and anyway she has freely admitted that, despite her Hollywood years, 'the stage has always had a first love-call on my heart'.

She read the script again. It finally *did* stick in her ribs and she agreed to play. She backed her confidence by putting up £8,000 of her own money as an investment in it and soon they were on the road. They travelled in better style than the last time Ginger and her mother were on tour, in the bygone 'two-to-five-a-day' vaudeville shows, but Ginger somehow had the same feeling of adventure. She even dug up the old coffee-pot that she carried with her on tour in the early days and took that along for the ride. It wouldn't surprise me to learn that it was smuggled somewhere in the luggage she brought for her trip to London for *Mame*.

The departure of Ginger from Hollywood after such a long time naturally caused a flutter of excitement around the old home town. One reporter asked her 'Why are you doing it? Why are you leaving all this . . .' and he jerked a vague hand in the direction of the swimming pool and the view, and possibly took in the Beverly Hills Hotel, that ritzy monument to the Golden Days of Hollywood. The reporter made it sound as though she might be planning a trip to the Antarctic instead of New Haven, Washington and Broadway.

'I'm doing it for fun,' she replied, 'there's nothing Freudian about it. If the audiences like the play then we'll all have a splendid, honest-to-goodness ball.' The reporter went away with a puzzled air. Ginger was far too uncomplicated for him; he was not used to meeting a film star who had never had occasion to hire her pet psychoanalyst—and hasn't heeded to do so to this day.

But *Love and Let Love* met with problems. There were things that were wrong with it, though nothing serious; it is to put these errors right that shows go out on pre-Broadway tours. In this instance, though, there was a lot of feudin' and fussin'. 'Getting Louis to change a line of his dialogue was like trying to change the Bible,' Ginger ruefully told Richard Coe of the *New York Times*. Still, though some of the critical reaction was a bit sniffy, the public came in. Maybe they came in more to see 'Ginger Rogers of Hollywood—In Person' than to see the play, but they seemed to enjoy it and box-offices were busy.

'Will you take it in to Broadway?' asked Coe.

Ginger's eyes widened. 'Of course. Why not? If I'm going to be a sitting duck I might as well sit for the big guns.'

Then she broke off and pealed with laughter as she showed the reporter one of the out-of-town reviews. It praised Ginger Rogers in one of the roles, but indicated that in the writer's opinion the part of the sister was played by an even better actress, a young woman named Virginia McMath—which was how the programme read.

'But never mind the critics,' remarked Ginger to Coe. 'They have their job to do—and let them do it. I'll do mine. The public will come,' she said confidently.

In retrospect, Ginger was over-confident. The play, apparently, was weak. At first people flocked to it, but it was obviously the attraction of Ginger Rogers the film star rather than the play, which did not fare well and soon disappeared from the Broadway scene. After the first night, critic Brooks Atkinson wrote this compliment to Ginger: 'She is beautiful and alive and also has a sunny sense of humour—no one that gorgeous can be actually overwhelmed by a playwright's dullness.'

There was no lamentation from Ginger, except a natural sadness when the combination of many talents fails to succeed. 'I've learned a great deal,' spoke the seasoned trouper. She had invested time and money (which, of course, she lost) but against that she had sniffed the atmosphere of the stage again; she had known for a while the joy of working in closer proximity to other people and in less clinical surroundings than a film studio.

More important, she had built up a rapport with audiences again. You can easily forget, if you are a film star, that you are being paid fabulously to make a depressed person laugh, a tired one think, to make people happy, tingle, even weep a little, just for a brief spell. In a film you act. You satisfy the director and the cameraman—and sometimes even yourself. The result of your work is looked at by accountants, top executives and the producer. Once they are satisfied, it is shipped across to the editor, on whose skill largely depends what film gets into the picture and what gets lost on the floor. The sound people, the music people, a hundred and one characters including the publicity department, the advertising men, the distributors, the exhibitors, all chip in with their ideas.

In the fullness of time, the film is unrolled in a cinema, and the star is probably making a film in Hawaii or Huddersfield or the Himalayas. The film is like last week's newspaper; the audience is a million light years away. The star does not hear their laughter or watch them being moved, and so he does not know of his mistakes or errors of judgment until far too late.

In the theatre, he knows at once. He can sense instant success or instant disaster by the mood of the house. He can react.

Ginger Rogers bought herself a refresher course for a mere £8,000 and some weeks away from her beloved house. It was cheap at the price. Besides, being Ginger, she also had fun. It seems she usually does.

Back in Hollywood, refreshed and eager to get started again, Ginger signed to make three films for 20th Century-Fox in 1952 which fully answered those who thought that she must have retired from filming simply because she had returned to flirt with her old love, the stage.

The first was *We're Not Married*, one of those episodic comedy-dramas which enable the company to stuff the film with star names since none of them works for more than a few days and it doesn't cost nearly so much as the cast-list makes it sound. In this instance, apart from Ginger, there were such attractive names as the fast rising Marilyn Monroe, Victor Moore, Eve Arden, Paul Douglas, Fred Allen, Mitzi Gaynor, David Wayne and that chatty extrovert, Zsa Zsa Gabor.

It seemed that Victor Moore as an ageing Justice of the Peace had married five couples while his licence was invalid. Consternation all round. Ginger and Fred Allen grabbed the best of the episodes, a sharp, ironic and witty anecdote about the effect the mistake could have on their radio programme, in which they played a happily married couple who gab and goo at breakfast time. They made a neat, tart team and it was a useful comedy film for Ginger.

Ginger's next effort was not so hot, though she was directed by Howard Hawks and had those two masterly comedians, Cary Grant and the veteran Charles Coburn, as co-stars. But any film—especially a comedy—called *Monkey Business* just had to be compared with the original Marx Brothers frolic some 20 years earlier. Not that it was even a remake or a wild distortion of the old film. It is simply that if the subject crops up among middle-aged film enthusiasts I will wager plenty that it is the Marx Brothers picture that springs to memory. You can't beat a legend. The Hawks comedy was one of those 'ain't life gland' frolics, in which Cary Grant played a research chemist who hit upon a formula for making people grow younger. He and his wife, Ginger, both tried it out and so, eventually, did most of the stars in the film. The gags and the situations in this film should have been given a stiff dose of the Grant formula.

Much more amusing was *Dreamboat*, in which she starred with the irascible, haughty Clifton Webb and Anne Francis. One can sympathize with Ronald Reagan, in his present exalted political position, when he is constantly reminded on television of mediocre films that he made as an averagely successful Hollywood actor.

In a minor way this was Webb's problem in *Dreamboat*. He was an actor whose former co-star, Ginger Rogers, insisted on featuring their old films on her television programme, to Webb's embarrassment. Just how the now dignified professor and Ginger came to terms over the problem resulted in a pleasant, light-hearted entertainment.

With *Dreamboat* safely in the can, and with two or three months before she was due to make *Forever Female* for Paramount, Ginger decided to take one of her rare holidays. She also decided to go to Europe, a strange decision, for Ginger, the All-American Gal, had never travelled much outside her own vast country. But late in 1952 she found herself on the Riviera, and a fateful trip it was to be.

Even the Riviera has its drawbacks when one is alone, and Ginger moved up quickly to Paris, that city about which more romantic guff has been spilled in lyrics, song and print than almost any other city one can name.

But for Ginger the romance was suddenly there, revealing itself at a party on the Left Bank where she met a stalwart, debonair young man with the right features, the right physique and the very right Gallic charm. It was evident that Jacques Bergerac was bedazzled by the radiance and vivacity of the gay Ginger. She was equally entranced by this well-mannered young Frenchman who made no secret of his admiration for her. And the Continental setting was made to measure.

They slipped away from the party and had their own party at Maxim's. The knowing old moon glinted over the Eiffel Tower, recognizing the evergreen symptoms. Then they moved on to Nice and Cannes; to Venice; to Capri; to various other spots clearly designed for no other purpose than as a background to burgeoning love affairs. When Ginger had to return to California to start work, Jacques quickly followed her, to Ginger's delight, for she is one who loves to be loved and be in love, and once again, ingenuously, Ginger was convinced that 'this was it'—that she had found her life partner.

Jacques had been a hotel clerk, had studied drama and was an established lawyer. It all seemed perfect. The one snag, on which the Hollywood werewolf columnists quickly pounced, was that Ginger was now nearing 42 and the new love of her life was only 26. Hollywood, remembering that three previous marriages had crashed round Ginger, tut-tutted censoriously. The objective outsider must have thought that this was one romance that had the odds stacked against it from the start.

GINGER—Salute to a Star

Ginger, an independent person, ignored all the chatter. She pulled a string or two and M.G.M. signed up her Romeo on a try-out contract at £50 a week, while he 'went to school' and learned something about film acting and what makes a studio tick.

She started her film at Paramount with William Holden. Based on a short play called *Rosalind* by Sir James Barrie, *Forever Female* turned out to be a brightly amusing story of an ageing actress who utterly refused to admit that she was getting older. Then a playwright (Holden) wrote a play for a young, fresh girl played by Patricia Crowley, and Ginger's eyes were opened. She realized that she was no longer an ingénue.

The gossip hounds snidely latched on to this in connection with Ginger's romance. Did she realize that *she* was no longer an ingénue? Still the couple ignored the cracks and were seen constantly, openly and happily together.

Forever Female was finished and was to create its own little niche in film history in November as the first feature film to have its première on television. It was shown as an attraction on the new Telemeter system at Palm Springs and viewers at home could see it for $1.35. Ginger was always way in ahead with experiments.

For Ginger there was an earlier and more important event at Palm Springs. She and Jacques Bergerac married there on February 7th, 1953. The tongues really started to wag then as the know-alls went into the familiar 'it can't possibly last' routine.

Said Jacques: I don't care what the press says. A few years either way—it doesn't matter if you are happy!

Said Ginger: When you're happy you don't count the years—in the same way that you don't count calories when you eat. I'll always be 15 days older than Jacques.

Said Jacques: Look at her—isn't she wonderful?

Said Ginger: Look at him—isn't he like a Greek God?

Said the world: But over 15 years' difference in their ages!

French polish

The gossip died down. The two were so obviously in love that even the most narrow-eyed scandal seekers had to admit themselves defeated; they turned to other sources for their chatter.

The two settled down to a quiet life, mostly spent at home, a life which even Hollywood (which can be as bigoted as any village community) could not fault. Jacques studied at the Metro studio and Ginger reported at 20th Century-Fox to make *Black Widow*. They rarely went out, but entertained quietly at home; they swam, played a lot of tennis and Ginger spent hours at her painting and at archery, a new craze with her. Ginger planned the meals and shopped at the Farmers' Market in Los Angeles. (Note to rubberneck tourists: that is where you will run into the stars if you wish to.) Occasionally they would go out to dinner and on to dance at a night spot. One oddity was that the two slept most nights in the open air. It was Jacques's idea ('it is healthy and romantic', he said) and as a loving, dutiful wife Ginger fell in with the idea and got to enjoy it. Or maybe, as a loving, dutiful wife, she pretended that she did.

It was around now that Ginger began to toy with an idea which was to shake a lot of people and send a buzz of conjecture through film circles.

But first Ginger was due to make *Black Widow*. It was a whodunit melodrama and Ginger was delighted that for once she would get the chance of being the villainess of the piece. Nunnally Johnson was to produce and direct and he also wrote the screenplay, and as boss of this one-man band he went to town by hiring a first class cast.

As well as Ginger there were Van Heflin, Gene Tierney, Otto Kruger, George Raft (for once on the side of the law), Reginald Gardiner, Cathleen Nesbitt and pretty Peggy Ann Garner. With a solid bunch of professionals like that everybody had to be on their toes, which is just as Ginger has always liked it.

Once again she was cast as an actress, a somewhat snooty,

imperious Broadway star. The story centred round who
strangled a young writer, played by Peggy Ann Garner.
Suspicion pointed at several people and how detective Raft put
the pieces together and pinned the murder on to Ginger built
up to a tense and plausible mystery yarn with which Ginger
could be well satisfied.

By now Ginger considered that her idea could be put into
motion. Her handsome French husband had studied enough at
drama classes to warrant his first break in pictures. She arranged
to make her first film abroad—in England, for British Lion.
Jacques Bergerac was to appear in it, with his wife, Stanley
Baker, Herbert Lom and Margaret Rawlings.

Eyebrows were raised. It looked a glaring example of influence. Since Ginger also invested some money in the film it was
probably not all that difficult to persuade the company to give
Jacques the role.

Ginger answered her critics crisply: 'I've found talent before
and it has succeeded. Jacques can do so as well.' She admitted,
though, that she had quietly told the producer that her husband
would be good in the role. Bergerac insisted firmly that he
didn't get the part through Ginger's influence. 'Film producers
don't give away parts like that,' he said rather defiantly when
he arrived in England. They do though, often. It depends on a
variety of circumstances.

At first glance it certainly looked a case of sentiment swaying
sense. On the other hand, Ginger was experienced and shrewd.
She *had* to believe that Jacques could play the role or she would
never have risked endangering the picture. Yet she also must
have known that, in his first film, Jacques was on trial and the
whole film world was looking on, a large section of it very
cynically.

The film, first called *Lifeline*, then *Twist of Fate* and finally
Beautiful Stranger, had a B-picture plot, but was given quite a
gloss by director David Miller and a Riviera background, which
could hardly have been more apt considering where Ginger

and Jacques had courted. She played an ex-actress (what, again?) and Jacques a young potter with whom Ginger got involved before discovering that Stanley Baker, her fiancé, was a dangerous criminal, mixed up in smuggling and all kinds of dirty deeds.

The film got away to a bad start when Wolf Rilla was dropped from the cast by mutual consent. Said Mr. Rilla, a shade bitterly: 'I thought I was supposed to act romantically with a girl of about 24 and even the glamorous Miss Rogers could hardly be taken for that.' What was really of interest was how the new boy would emerge from his first acting ordeal. Jacques Bergerac's role was far from demanding, but he had the good looks and the romantic virility to provide a vicarious thrill for most women in the cinemas.

Harold Conway, writing for the *Daily Sketch*, was not impressed. Describing the film as a 'childish rigmarole', he wrote that for years he had adored Ginger as Hollywood's most delectable and intelligent actress 'but it is going to take me years to forgive her for this. I must assume that Ginger offered herself as a sacrifice in return for her fourth husband being given a part in the film.' Conway continued: 'M. Bergerac brings to his screen début a luxuriant thatch of hair, a classic Roman profile—and an air of dedicated attachment to his leading lady which bears no identifiable resemblance to acting. Miss Rogers herself acts like fury to provide ballast. But while his co-performers are sinking, Herbert Lom takes refuge in wild burlesque and imperturbably floats as an eccentric confidence-trickster.'

Not very happy words and the film turned out to be a tepid misfire. Yet Ginger was content. Her husband was launched on his career and she felt her confidence was justified, even in this novelettish picture. Time has partially proved her right, for Jacques has remained an actor, albeit not a very distinguished one. The man who much later was to marry Dorothy Malone, star of television's *Peyton Place*, could look Hollywood straight in the eyes when they returned: no longer a student, but an embryo actor.

The two enjoyed themselves in England, where they made friends and people seemed glad that their marriage appeared to be working out on an even keel, with the age barrier seemingly unimportant. The spell in Europe also gave them a respite from the bitchy backbiting and innuendoes of the often spiteful and envious Hollywood colony.

Back in Hollywood, Ginger, with hair blonder than usual and cut short (because Jacques liked it better that way), and in her usual sharp physical trim—132 lb, 26-inch waist, $35\frac{1}{2}$-inch bust and $37\frac{1}{2}$-inch hips, which have been her approximate comely measurements for years—decided on a fresh challenge. Television.

Back in 1951 she had reportedly signed a television contract for £360,000 to make a half-hour TV programme each week for five years, but nothing seemed to have come of that handsome offer. Still, Ginger was happy. Her marriage seemed safe, more films were in the offing, and even the loss of a mink coat and other possessions when she was staying at Great Fosters in England hardly perturbed her. Philosophically Ginger remarked: 'Things like minks never bring real happiness. I'm sure the thieves are far more worried than I am.'

It was in this cheerful state of mind that, towards the end of the year, Ginger broke into television, making her début in a programme called *Showcase*, which, directed by the temperamental Otto Preminger, consisted of three one-act plays by Noël Coward. Ilka Chase, Gloria Vanderbilt and Margaret Hayes were also in the production.

Showcase it was called and showcase it was, giving Ginger a neat chance to prove her versatility. She played the castoff wife in *Shadow Play* (another dream role, ironically, for the very down-to-earth Miss Rogers), the wife in *Still Life* and, in striking contrast, half of a husband-wife variety song-and-patter act in *Red Peppers*. For this she earned the handsome sum of £6,000 plus. The contrast in Ginger's three performances, notably as the wistful wife in *Still Life* and the ebullient, red-nosed, sharp-tongued hoofer in *Red Peppers*, was quite outstanding, according to friends of mine who saw the show in America, and marked her out once again as one of Hollywood's best talents.

Later Ginger was to appear in most of the top television shows, usually as a guest artist. She made many appearances with the swift-tongued Bob Hope, Dinah Shore, Perry Como, Jack Benny, Ed Sullivan, Pat Boone, Red Skelton and in *Hollywood Palace*, and many others welcomed her in their spectaculars; for Pontiac she made her own spectacular. Virginia Mason, a West End dancer and choreographer, appeared in this Pontiac spectacular with Ginger and told me: 'She was a most pleasant person to work with. She was a fairly slow study and so had to work and rehearse tirelessly for the show. She never seemed to tire or get frayed; I was tremendously impressed by her energy and enthusiasm.' Yet television has never tempted Ginger away from the big screen; the cinema was always the backbone of her career.

Witty, razor-edge dialogue and tense situations were the hallmark of Ginger's next film, *Tight Spot*, which turned out to be one of the best films she had made since the war. The film was based on a taut crime play called *Dead Pigeon* and Ginger was cast as a tough, hard-bitten gangster's moll taken out of jail and set up by the police to turn state evidence against a bigtime hoodlum.

Her scenes with Edward G. Robinson as the District Attorney and with Brian Keith, the policeman detailed as her bodyguard, were gripping and astringent. (Said Ginger to Keith: 'You men are all alike. You've only got different faces so we can tell you apart.') Ginger delivered such dialogue with the same adept sureness that she could use to whip up a laugh in a flippant comedy role; her deftness had the same sharp timing and placing as that of an ace tennis champion.

Her next stint was *The First Travelling Saleslady*, a turn-of-the-century comedy which had originally been planned as a comeback for Mae West, but when plans were switched Ginger happily took over. It meant that she would be returning to the RKO studio, scene of her Oscar victory and the goldspun dancing series with Fred Astaire, for the first time in ten years. Employees who had been at RKO during the Astaire-Rogers regime went all out to give her a welcome back.

Taking on films originally designed for another actress happened several times to Ginger, but as a trouper she regarded it as the luck of the draw. If things went wrong she never whimpered afterwards that the proposition was not really meant for her. She wasn't forced to take the film, was she? No. Then, figured Ginger, let's get on with it and give it all we've got. But this time it wasn't enough.

She threw a big party to mark Carol Channing's début in films. Carol, a tall, funny girl, and Ginger were surrounded by tall, stalwart leading men to make Carol feel that she was not dwarfing six-footers like Barry Nelson, James Arness, Clint Eastwood and David Brian. But the comedy, in which Ginger as a corset saleslady went West and secretly sold barbed wire to the homesteaders, was laboured, though there were plenty of amusing moments. Ginger did not care either for having to wear tightly laced corsets; her trim figure rebelled at the unexpected restraint.

She was relieved to move on to her next film, *Teenage Rebel*, a neatly contrived comedy with Michael Rennie, Mildred Natwick and a new young girl named Betty Lou Keim. I thought the picture was over sentimental, but it provided some sound performances. It was a peek, cloying at times, perceptive at others, at the problems of a sensitive child when her parents are divorced. Not that young Miss Keim seemed particularly sensitive. In a remarkable performance, which makes one wonder why her career apparently faded out, she played an insufferable sulky brat, and Ginger and Michael Rennie, as her new husband, kept their sense of humour amazingly well in the circumstances.

Ginger was frequently lumbered with such appalling lines as 'I had no idea that Dorothy's father would use the little girl I adored to punish me'—enough to make the most avid Rogers fan swiftly seek the exit. The reviews were mixed. Jympson Harman of the *Evening News* begged Ginger to 'be her age'. He gallantly claimed that 'she looked 25 and far too young to be the mother of a 15-year-old'. Roy Nash of the *Star* proclaimed Ginger's legs as 'still among the wonders of the world', but others were less kind about the film. 'Gruesome exercise in maternal sentimentality,' snorted the *Manchester Guardian*. 'Ginger seemed a vapid mother to rouse sympathy,' sighed *Time;* while Philip Oakes, in the *Standard*, wrote: 'Ginger Rogers wades through the mush with her chin held high' and one can but assume that he was paying her a heavy-handed compliment.

Perhaps Ginger's mind was not for once entirely on her job, for there was persistent gossip that the stardust was shining less than bright on her own idyllic marriage to Jacques Bergerac. The spiky tongue of rumour was hinting that the romantic Gallic actor was casting interested eyes in the direction of the petite actress Phyllis Kirk, and that the looks were not un-reciprocated.

Ginger went on a Services tour with Bob Hope's company to Alaska; Jacques went to Mexico for the opening of the Hilton Hotel. 'Whether he will come back I don't know,' she told reporter Jonah Ruddy. 'We've had quarrels and disagreements and I would do anything to avoid them. Quarrels have a terrible effect on me.'

The two were divorced in July 1957, after four years, five months. Ginger claimed that he was mentally cruel; that he drove too fast though he knew she hated it; that he would go for days without speaking to her, except on occasional necessary 'Yes' or 'No'; that he would read French classics out loud in front of her guests at parties. She claimed no alimony. The song was over. For both of them the melody had been splendid for a long time but it went off tune.

What happened is nobody's business but theirs. Some think that Ginger tried to 'remake' the young Frenchman and remember the determined comment she is reported to have made when they were married. 'I'll show them,' she is supposed to have said, referring to those who were knocking the chances of the marriage almost before the confetti was out of their hair. Jacques was briefly non-committal. He said: 'We have a different approach to life.'

With Dan Dailey, David Niven, Barbara Rush, Tony Randall and Ginger in the cast the Nunnally Johnson film of *Oh Men! Oh Women!* should have been a riotous light comedy, an inconsequential piece of lighthearted nonsense bordering round a psychiatrist's consulting room. It turned out to be flat-footed, the fun too contrived. It was to be the last film that Ginger was to make for seven years.

Ginger's decision to leave the cinema for a while was a considered one. It did not mean, as some people too quickly decided, that she was finished in show business. 'Retire?' she once said, in wide eyed surprise. 'What do they expect me to do. Sit around and knit?'

But consider the facts. She was rich and was not forced to work unless an assignment fully interested her. She had worked hard and long since she was little more than a child and had met all the taxing demands of studios and stardom. She had plenty of other interests to occupy her agile mind and energetic body. Moreover, she was sensible enough to face up to the fact that some of the films she had become involved in during the past two or three years were cinematic stinkers. She was prepared to wait until something came along worthy of her interest and her prestige. It was her choice that it became such a long wait.

Meanwhile, she turned her attention to what was for her a

new venture. She went into cabaret as a café singer. She opened with four dancers—The Toppers—in a 40-minute act at the Riviera Club in Havana. Her appearances in television spectaculars, notably with the quiet, languid singer, Perry Como, suggested that the night club act would be tremendous.

She was carried on by the boys and looked a dream, first in a wine-coloured gown and then in gold lamé which perfectly matched her sparkle. She sang and danced with verve. But José, who covered the Havana beat for *Variety*, sadly reported: 'Not much of Ginger Rogers came through.'

Her act had been written by that witty writer-performer, Kay Thompson, and unfortunately there was more Thompson than Rogers in the routine. She turned her back on the past and what she gave the customers, pleasant enough though it was, entertained them but did not lift them on to Cloud Nine. What they wanted were nostalgic reminders of the songs and dances that had made the Astaire-Rogers pictures so magical.

Ginger took stock again and once more she was attracted to the theatre; she toured in summer stock with that zingy musical comedy, *Bells Are Ringing*. It was a bright, boisterous show about a girl running a private telephone answering system who gets mixed up with a bunch of gangsters. It had been a great Broadway success for Judy Holliday, who later filmed it with Dean Martin. The zany heroine was completely up Ginger's street; it had humour, romance and lively numbers and her vivacious attack delighted audiences. Ginger was equally delighted to be back among the bustle of the theatre, with the smell of grease paint and the personal feeling of rapport with human beings, backstage or front. She just likes people.

Ginger was talking like a true stage trouper when she once said: 'Audiences can't fail to be more exhilarating than a camera peering down your throat.' She was then about to return to the theatre in *Love And Let Love*. 'Maybe,' she added, 'audiences will be like a vitamin to me.'

GINGER—Salute to a Star

The bells pealed gaily for Ginger but people then expected that she would soon be back in front of the cameras. Wisely, Ginger decided that she could wait. Out of the clear blue sky, the BBC invited her to London to star in one of their most lavish holiday television attractions. They wanted her for the TV show, *Carissima*, a musical comedy romance written by Eric Maschwitz and Hans May. Remember Maschwitz's shows, which included *Balalaika*, *New Faces*, *Paprika* and *Summer Song?* and 'A Nightingale Sang In Berkeley Square' and 'These Foolish Things' were among his most memorable songs.

Carissima had run for 466 performances at the Palace Theatre ten years or so earlier and had been lavishly and expensively staged. In celebration Eric and his wife, Phyl Gordon, who were then running the Gay Nineties, an elegant little West End club much favoured by the rich and the near-rich, introduced a new cocktail called simply 'Carissima'.

A curious columnist—me—wondered why the sophisticated Maschwitz had so naïvely and with seemingly unusual lack of subtlety named a cocktail after his new show. It seemed far too obvious. I had forgotten to translate the title and had under-estimated Maschwitz's devious wit. Said Eric: 'If you can't guess then you must buy a round. It means what it is called—"Carissima", dearest of all.' I bought a round; Eric was painfully right.

The BBC engagement and the trip to London were both keenly anticipated by Ginger; yet the anticipation was tinged with a slight wariness. Her last visit had been to make the film *Beautiful Stranger* with her new husband, Jacques Bergerac. Ginger somehow got the impression that both at the press reception and on visits to the film set the press was trying to needle her. For her taste, there were far too many references to the disparity in age between herself and her new groom. She had forgotten that a marriage between a screen darling in her forties and a 26-year-old, good-looking Frenchman about to star in his first film—and possibly introduced into it by her influential contacts with Hollywood's upper strata—was a newspaper story in anybody's terms.

I am not being chauvinistic when I write that in my view none of my colleagues has ever been quite so virulent and bitchy about any star as have some of Hollywood's Queen Bees of the press. Do you want examples? No. The she-dragons thrive well enough without the publicity.

This time she was alone; the marriage was over. However, if Ginger thought that people would steamroller through their interviews she must have been pleasantly surprised. The question of age and the broken marriage cropped up, naturally. She must have expected that. But nobody bullied or was snide and nobody wanted to be, because who wants to get tough with people who are cordial and frank when answering questions? There are some Hollywood stars, of course, with whom it is a case of the winner being the one who gets in the first dirty crack. Even newspapermen are entitled to protect themselves against ill-mannered, jumped-up bigheads.

Britain was glad to see Ginger for that Whit Monday television treat. She was being paid around £2,500 for rehearsals and the one night show. The only writer who was sour about that pleasant sounding figure had not done his homework. He had forgotten that in the States Ginger rated around £1,000 for a single *guest* performance on a top variety show. He also forgot that out of her BBC fee she had to pay fares, hotels and, I was told, the cost of her clothes. If the latter is true then Ginger should have had a bitter slanging match with her agent or manager; a show like *Carissima* could scarcely be dressed out of a woman's normal wardrobe.

Alas, the show was bad. Philip Purser, TV critic of the *News Chronicle*, acidly summed it up as : 'Mediocrissima'. There were some complimentary notices, mainly for Ginger playing a non-singing, non-dancing role which Shirl Conway, a popular young American, originally played at the Palace. There was little applause for the expensive flop of a show.

Miss Rogers, the pro-supremo, did not wilt under the experience. She said: 'I suppose I should have had my head examined. We should all have had our heads examined. Back home in the States we have a minimum of a week's rehearsal for every 30 minutes of the show, and this one ran for 90 minutes. Here we had two erratic weeks' rehearsal. Less than that really, because the show was written ten years before and needed plenty of updating.' She smiled, with one of those what-the-hell-that's-show-business grins, and added: 'While the rewriting was being tossed around there wasn't much chance to rehearse seriously.' Here the experienced pro took over again: 'I wouldn't trade in the experience for anything.'

Obviously she did not learn much in the acting line. But part of the business of survival in the show-business jungle is to note and register methods, problems, shortcomings. So this was the BBC splashing out on a super production? I would guess that the chance of the BBC getting Ginger Rogers to star in a television musical while playing in *Mame* would be minimal. Forgetting any possible contractual barriers, I can visualize her warily avoiding another *Carissima* setback.

She was due to go home. She admitted that she still loved Jacques Bergerac but didn't know whether she could ever take him back. She cleared up any misunderstandings about her previous trip. All was happy and a newspaperman spoke for everyone when he wrote: 'There's still a lot of Ginger in Miss Rogers.'

It was to be a better trip home. On her flight to Britain the plane had developed engine trouble in the Arctic and had to land at an unbelievably inclement and lonely outpost on Banff Island, with the noon temperature clocking zero. She was warmed though when a young reporter, doubtless regarding this as his finest moment, described Ginger as 'one of the most beautiful women I have ever met.'

Sir Charles Cochran, a connoisseur both professionally and privately of magnificent women, had previously spiked the

French polish

young man's guns. Years before, Cochran had described Ginger Rogers as '*the* most beautiful woman I have ever seen.' An impresario, a reporter and millions of fans all over the world can hardly be wrong, can they?

When Ginger got back to the States she still had no desire to return to the cinema, which naturally had altered a great deal since the war but, thought Ginger, not necessarily for the better. The theatre still excited her more.

She went into a show called *The Pink Jungle*, and started a tour with a view to Broadway. Let this sad effort rest in peace. It finished with abject abruptness in Boston and the impresarios said that it was being taken off while it was given a 'face lift.' Ginger remarked acidly: 'It needs more than a face lift. They had better bury it.'

They did.

Chapter 9

AGAIN—THE LULLABY
OF BROADWAY

As the 1960's rolled in Ginger was happily 'rediscovering' the legitimate stage. She decided to go on the road.

This has a somewhat different connotation from a stint on tour in Britain. Often the latter merely means that a show is being tried out before it goes to the West End, or is marking time until a West End theatre is available. It can often be merely a final attempt to squeeze a few more drops out of the box-office orange. 'Direct From Its Great West End Run' is often simply an alibi for the last, dying gasps of a show that has just about outworn its welcome in Shaftesbury Avenue.

In America, there are National Tours, summer stock and 'bus-and-truck' tours. A National Tour will play several weeks at each of several key centres outside New York; summer stock is roughly the equivalent of repertory seasons in Britain; 'bus-and truck' tours are lesser trips around the circuits, penetrating places which the main railway routes do not always cover. The cast then travels by bus, accompanied by the scenery, costumes and props in trucks.

A National Tour may follow a Broadway run or even play other cities in the vast States while the Broadway show is still flourishing. It will play to different audiences from those who frequent Broadway's 'expense account avenue', and will be cast with stars of equal calibre to those playing in Manhattan.

Again—the lullaby of Broadway

Ginger went on National Tours with *Annie Get Your Gun*, *Bell, Book and Candle* and *The Unsinkable Molly Brown*. She was particularly eager to play in *Annie*. She had wanted very much to capture the film role of Annie Oakley, the hoydenish Wild West sharpshooter who gave her name to at least one bit of theatrical lore; to this day free theatre tickets are described as 'Annie Oakleys' or 'Annies'. 'I really wanted that part desperately,' Ginger has confessed. 'I would have played it for a dollar just to make it contractually legal.' But the part went to Betty Hutton. Betty played it well, I thought, but rather too much on one key.

I have seen no less than seven different actresses play Annie, even including one very good amateur in a bank operatic company and also a sterling performance by Barbara Shotter, a little-known British actress. I would say that it is difficult to fail in this meaty part if you know your stuff as a musicomedy actress.

Has there been any musical since the war—even *My Fair Lady*—with such a wealth of songs, nearly all show-stoppers, as this Irving Berlin musical fiesta? 'Anything You Can Do', 'Doin' what Comes Naturally', 'No Business Like Show Business', 'You Can't Get A Man With A Gun', 'The Girl That I Marry'—the list of great songs is endless. No wonder Ginger coveted the role. I only wish I had seen her play it, even on the night at Rhode Island when she fell into the orchestra pit from a bike and had to assure the audience that she was in one piece.

On and off she played in *Annie* and the other two shows for about three years. At the Vogue Terrace Theatre, Pittsburgh, she found herself playing it to an audience of some 700 on an open stage without a curtain, with horseshoe-shaped ramps at either end and another ramp down centre stage.

For the first hour, wrote one critic, Ginger's small voice was swamped. Then she seemed to sum up her leading man, Bruce Yarnell, who was in particularly fine voice that night. Whether or not the words of one of the songs, 'Anything You Can Do I Can Do Better', challenged her I don't know. 'But suddenly,' wrote the critic, 'Ginger Rogers took over.'

Bell, Book and Candle was a sophisticated joke by John Van Druten, well suited to Ginger's vein of comedy, and *The Unsinkable Molly Brown* was a tuneful, tomboyish musical comedy, later turned into an M.G.M. film with Debbie Reynolds and Harve Presnel, an actor who, unlike Miss Brown, seems to have sunk without trace; at least I cannot recall seeing him on the screen since. The film was far from being sensational, but Ginger broke several house records with it on stage.

Meanwhile, the stop-press news was that Ginger was in love again. He was an actor-producer-writer whom she had known for some time and had been touring with her in *Bell, Book and Candle*. His name was William Marshall and, though some six or seven years younger than Ginger, he was a mature man of the world who had already been married twice, his ex-wives being two beautiful French actresses, Michèle Morgan and Micheline Presle. Ginger and Marshall tied the knot on March 17th, 1961; at the age of nearly 50 Ginger was setting out on her fifth bid for the elusive contentment in marriage for which she had always yearned. Bill Marshall had for some time been active in the show-business labyrinth and knew the score; the two had much to offer each other.

Though Ginger has never aspired to political activity she believes that actors have as much right and indeed duty to interest themselves in politics as any other citizens. Around this time, with the glow of her fifth marriage still lighting her up, she started a barnstorming campaign on behalf of the present president, Richard Nixon, who in 1962 was standing for the Governorship of California. Ginger toured around, urging Republican wives to 'come out of the kitchen and go to the backyard fence. You can't find out how to wash your clothes whiter unless you talk to your neighbours.'

I don't quite get the political subtlety of this message—it

seemed to suggest Mr. Nixon was a form of high-class detergent —but her active role in politics subsided somewhat as she and her husband became interested in another activity, the possibility of building up a film industry in Jamaica. At the time it was reported that they were selling up their Hollywood home and their two ranches and were to emigrate to Jamaica to build studios and create a new Hollywood.

As so often happens in Hollywood, an acorn of truth became a forest of conjecture and misapprehension. They claimed later that there was never any solid intention of trying to build up a big-time industry. They merely hoped to acquire or rent a studio. There they would take advantage of what they figured could be ideal film-making conditions: the warm, balmy climate, beautiful scenery and low financial costs all being attractive to their plan.

The idea, so far, is virtually stillborn. William Marshall Productions has made only one film, *The Confession*, starring Ginger as the madame of an Italian whore-house. Ray Milland, Cecil Kellaway, Michael Azzara, Carl Schell and Barbara Eden were also in the film, and it was directed by William Dieterle, who several years earlier had solemnly assured me that he was going to retire after his next film. The Rogers-Marshall picture was finished in 1964 but has not yet seen the light of day and there is no indication of whether or not it will ever be released.

Ginger returned and became involved in a film which was her 73rd and, at present, her last. I do not believe it will be her last; I most sincerely hope not.

Four or five years ago a colourful, unsavoury biography of that dazzlingly blonde, ill-fated screen actress Jean Harlow hit the bookstalls and garnered a lot of publicity. It probably inspired two biographical films about her.

Ginger appeared in an experimental film for Magna Pictures called *Harlow*. It was described as an Electrovision production. God made the earth in six days and on the seventh He rested; man, in his infinite wisdom and progress, has not yet found it possible to make a good feature film in a week. *Harlow* was shot in seven days—and looked it. Carol Lynley, portraying Miss Harlow, Barry Sullivan and Efrem Zimbalist were others hired—with Ginger—to bring in a quick job.

Ginger stole most of the notices as Jean Harlow's mother. Curiously, so did Angela Lansbury. She also played Mrs. Harlow in another film with the same title in which Carroll Baker was signed as the torrid Jean. This seems to prove nothing except, perhaps, that you have to be a seasoned pro like Angela or Ginger to salvage any little treasure that may lurk in a dustheap.

Shortly after she had finished *Harlow*, which turned out to be a tawdry, ill-advised experiment, Broadway beckoned again. Ginger was invited to take over from Carol Channing as the star of *Hello, Dolly!* which had opened with Carol Channing at St. James's Theatre in New York on January 16th, 1964. It was based on *The Matchmaker* by Thornton Wilder, which in turn had been derived from earlier farces including *The Merchant of Yonkers*.

Though the show had only one outstanding song—the title number—it was both funny and exhilarating, warm and artless. The role of Mrs. Dolly Levy, the woman who managed other people's love lives (for an appropriate fee) but found it far more tricky to promote her own matrimonial future, was an outstanding vehicle for an actress. Early in 1969 it became the longest running show on Broadway, with over 2,200 performances, and indeed was then the fifth longest running show in Broadway history. It had made about $8,000,000 profit in productions in many parts of the world—without including the film rights. In every way, *Hello, Dolly!* has been a gilt-edged hit.

It must have been an immediate temptation to Ginger to play in this phenomenal success but she demurred and, it is said, turned down the idea three times. It was not that she disliked either the show or the role, but she felt that Carol

Channing had made the part so much her own that following in her footsteps could only be an undue risk.

She under-estimated both *Hello, Dolly!* and her own drawing power. The part demanded a warm, outgiving personality, a shrewd sense of comedy—yet, withal, a capacity for sympathy, emotion and a flair for wearing colourful period costumes, qualities which Ginger possessed abundantly. She agreed to take over and was glad of her decision. She was a rousing success in a part that was subsequently to be played by Martha Raye, followed by Betty Grable and then Pearl Bailey in an all-coloured version with Cab Calloway. Dorothy Lamour—*sans* sarong—appeared in it on tour and when Ginger went out with it on the National Tour, after a long Broadway spell, she was once playing it for eight performances a week in Las Vegas with Dorothy Lamour doing it for six.

When Ginger took over from Miss Channing in August 1965 the critics, rightly, did not overdo comparison with her predecessor. No actress worthy of her greasepaint will ever give a carbon copy of another's performance. She had rehearsed for only three weeks before plunging into Broadway's hottest showcase, but she emerged with distinct honours.

Whitney Bolton, critic of the *Morning Telegraph*, summed up thus: 'Miss Rogers is talent, always has been, even back there in the thirties when she was a sprout making her first movies . . . she has the figure for those costumes . . . Miss Rogers was a noble inspiration when the wracking task of supplanting Miss Channing came along.'

The *New York Herald Tribune*'s man in the stalls, Stuart W. Little, declared: 'She looked happy as she came on stage to take over for Carol Channing and she had reason to be . . . Miss Rogers had the evening all wrapped up after a couple of scenes.'

The general feeling among the 'Butchers of Broadway' was that Ginger's interpretation was quieter than that of her predecessor but that she made her own niche in the history of

Hello, Dolly!, and Broadway theatregoers echoed the sentiment of the show's big song spot in thinking 'Hello, Ginger, it's so nice to have you back where you belong'.

And then came *Mame*, the comedy role which Angela Lansbury established before she switched over to open in *Dear World*. Ginger would have been very welcome had she decided to do another take-over and replace Miss Lansbury. However, Jayne Morgan and later that lithe, long-legged dancing film beauty Ann Miller did so, while Janet Blair was picked for the 'bus-and-truck' tour.

There were other plans for Ginger. In England Harold Fielding and Bernard Delfont were earmarking *Mame* for Drury Lane and preparing to lay siege to Ginger with the long, patient negotiations that were to bring her to London's top musical playhouse.

(*above*) In *Stage Door* (1937) with Katharine Hepburn and Adolphe Menjou (*below*) In *Bachelor Mother* (1939) with David Niven

Two scenes from *Kitty Foyle* (1940) (*above*) She plays a happy-go-lucky youngster with Ernest Cossart. (*below*) With Gladys Cooper and Dennis Morgan

(*above*) *Primrose Path* (1940) gave Ginger a strong dramatic role. Here she is with Joel McCrea. (*below*) *Roxie Hart* (1942) Ginger is telling Lynne Overman where he gets off, while check-capped Phil Silvers and others look on

In *The Major and the Minor* (1942) Ginger posed as a child to get half fare on a train and caused plenty of trouble for co-star Ray Milland

Chapter 10

GINGER—THE QUIET VISITOR

After all the starry palaver and beating of drums which Harold Fielding and his publicity aide, Roger Clifford, had helped to create to greet Ginger Rogers' arrival, people might have been forgiven for expecting that 'Swinging London' would be her oyster. They probably anticipated that she would be here, there and everywhere, seen at the right spots, doing 'the season', getting her photograph in the papers with all the 'right' people. Far from it: Ginger is not a night-club addict.

She had come to London to do a job and a very responsible one. When she arrived was there not already £260,000 of advance bookings, representing over 40 per cent of the theatre spread over 32 weeks? If you take your job seriously figures like that cannot be dismissed lightly. Ginger began to 'go into training', for she has often said that to be a star it is necessary to be as fit and dedicated as a champion boxer.

The day after her arrival there was a press conference, one of those crowded, fantastic occasions inseparable from show business. This was what the publicity man called a 'courtesy reception', to allow what seemed like 20,000 milling reporters, photographers, rubbernecks and waiters with drinks to bask in the presence of the star and the writers to ask what questions they could while the cameramen flashed their bulbs and clicked away for posterity. The chances of any newspapermen getting a coherent story in such scrimmages is always rather bleak, but they do serve one useful purpose. They enable journalists to observe the star's behaviour under fire.

Miss Rogers coped promptly, intelligently and sweetly with a myriad questions (most of which must have been old hat to her and many of which, in fact, she had answered only the day before to the journalists privileged to board the Mame Express). The consensus of opinion was that Ginger seemed 'a very okay girl'. She had passed the first test with honours.

Following this she went into retirement. She had work to do. *Mame* was already looming up. She and her husband spent Christmas at the country home of two old friends, agent Christopher Mann and his famous pianist wife, Eileen Joyce. From then on she was seen very little. Her social activities were confined to an occasional theatre and quiet, intimate meals with the Manns and other close friends.

She had little time even to paint, though to paint London's scene was the relaxation to which she was mainly looking forward. In any case, she expressed herself in rare interviews as slightly disenchanted with two aspects of London. 'It seems to have become boxy and New Yorky, with so many ugly new blocks of apartments,' she thought. 'And some of the new "skyscrapers" are surely spoiling the skyline?' she added. She was also outspoken about the rents that were being asked for apartments. Much as they liked the Savoy, Ginger and Bill Marshall wanted to get their own place to live while in London. They are home-birds and the 54 weeks for which she had provisionally signed for the show was quite a long spell.

Even after three or four months they had not found an apartment at a reasonable rent. ('One paper said I was willing to pay 315 guineas a week,' Judy Innes of the *Mail* reported her as saying. 'I may not be bright, but I'm not that stupid.') She found that estate agents were sadly underestimating the number and size of the bedrooms and bathrooms they needed for living space, luggage and guests. So, particularly in the early days, the star was far too busy house-hunting and preparing for *Mame* rehearsals to paint the town a pale pink, even if she had had the inclination.

Neither did Ginger keep cropping up on endless television and radio shows. *Mame* was—and always has been, since she first signed to play the role—her first and major concern. I stress this because she kept so much under cover that some people even suggested that she had changed her mind and gone back to the States!

Except for three or four newspapers the theatre in Britain is treated with scant interest by the press. Even a big, glittering first night often receives less attention than a Fourth Division soccer match. But the arrival of Ginger Rogers at Drury Lane Theatre for the first rehearsal of the new musical certainly pulled in the cameramen. The famous legs which the males on her arrival at Waterloo Station had good-humouredly pleaded to see were to be on view.

Ginger walked on to the Drury Lane stage; her blonde hair was flying loosely; she was wearing a gold tunic over black pants and sweater and, accompanied by dancers George May and David Wright, she danced her first steps on the famous boards—and looked as radiant and lithe as when she made her Broadway début in *Top Speed* nearly 40 years earlier. She high-kicked for the cameras and her breathing was as faultless as her steps. Her colleagues in the cast looked on and nodded approvingly; it was a critical audience, but they recognized genuine star quality. She went into some of the routines from the show and Lawrence Kasha, restaging the Broadway production, grinned confidently: 'Only trouble is that everyone's afraid to handle her—the chorus boys think she's made of glass and that they'll hurt her. But Ginger can take it.'

Then she disappeared to the ballet room and practised for an hour or so. No problem. Ever since her arrival she had been limbering up for two hours a day and singing for three, and she was raring to get started.

She eased up. There were still nearly six weeks to go before the string of previews arranged to break in the show before the official first night. Ginger moved into her 'film star' dressing room. This £2,000 super suite was just another much discussed phase of the remarkable campaign that Fielding and Delfont had agreed on to make the London début of Ginger Rogers something extra special.

As Fielding said: 'She'll be spending many hours a week in the theatre. We want her to feel at home.' So he hired designer Adam Pollock to dream up a suite that spelled Hollywood. Though Ginger said that it was smaller than the rooms she had for years at RKO studios, she agreed that it was 'just as pretty— and the prettiest I've ever seen in a theatre'. The suite had a personal bathroom and dressing room and a fully equipped kitchen. The main room was lined with nearly 200 yards of pink raw silk and the décor incorporated 6,000 pieces of squared glass. Dominating the room was a canopied couch in pale cream silk. There were white pedestals, silver satin lamp-shades and hand painted silver designs on the door frames.

Designer Pollock described the overall effect as 'a pink haze' —and he wasn't exaggerating. One visitor, visibly dazzled by the opulent effect, whispered to her companion: 'If I had a joint like this they'd have to drag me out of it to get me on stage!'

Extravagance on the part of Harold Fielding? Not a bit to anyone who recognizes that showmanship is an essential art in giving a show that extra spark that fills seats. The £2,000 he spent on redecorating Ginger's 'theatre home' not only paid off as a setting to make his star feel on top of the world but also more than paid off in publicity. It was but a small bite out of the £100,000 which he and Bernard Delfont had put up to stage in Britain a show that has already grossed a sizable fortune in the United States.

The money went in advertising, publicity stunts and travel and hotel expenses for the Americans who came over to restage

Ginger—the quiet visitor

Mame for Drury Lane; £10,000 was spent in paying musicians and the company for rehearsals long before the show opened; £45,000 was lashed out on décor and dresses and designs— Ginger's 22 costumes alone set back Fielding and his partner £15,000. Fielding told Brian Dean of the *Daily Mail* that around £10,000 was absorbed in 'a hundred and one things which go towards a show—such as orchestrations, transatlantic phone calls, insurance premiums and so on.'

Ginger's salary would be over and above all that and come out of box-office receipts. As she left Drury Lane Theatre on that first full day of work on the new venture there was a comforting queue at the box-office. Harold Fielding and Ginger were in business.

Several nights before the official opening the charity premières began, designed primarily to give the cast the 'feel' of the show and to provide word-of-mouth publicity for it. Princess Margaret, Lord Snowdon and Princess Alexandra were among those who had an advance look at the show, as well as a range of glittering and influential people who, if they liked the show, could give it a great start even before the first night. They did like it.

Ginger Rogers, Ann Beach, Barry Kent, Margaret Courtenay, Burt Kwouk, Guy Spaull, young Gary Warren and the rest of a cast of around 26 principals and a score of dancers and singers awoke on February 20th, 1969 knowing that 'this is the night'. The theatre had that air of expectancy that always accompanies a first night, especially one that has been launched with expertise and promises glitter, colour, fun and a star for whom the entire audience would have an affection born of nostalgia or about whom they would feel a keen but equally affectionate curiosity. The entrance to Drury Lane Theatre was a bower of flowers and a special carpet inscribed 'Mame' had been laid to welcome the guests. Huge cars and taxis sleekly pulled up.

The crowds who always assemble for these 'special occasions' were busy spotting the faces they could name: regular first-nighters and those drawn by the 'in-the-swim' determination not to miss a notable night, and nearly all for once dressed to kill—no longer a certainty at theatre first nights.

The millionaires, the socialites, the young men about town and stars such as Ben Lyon and Bebe Daniels, who had filmed with Ginger in the early days, Dame Edith Evans, Stanley Baker, David Hemmings, Roger Moore, Sandie Shaw—all helped to make up one of the most starry, celebrity-studded audiences since *My Fair Lady* opened at the same theatre.

To some *Mame* was a new experience; far more remembered Beatrice Lillie playing the straight version of Patrick Dennis's book at the Adelphi 11 years earlier and Rosalind Russell's fine performance on the screen. But this night it was Ginger's task to bring to life, in a glamorous new setting, the eccentric, Bohemian aunt who, entrusted with the education of her nephew, a ten-year-old orphan, was to 'open new doors of experience' for the lad. Few in the theatre wished her anything but a rollicking success.

The orchestra struck up, the lights went down and, as John Barber of the *Daily Telegraph* wrote: 'The legendary lady swept down a spiral staircase on the centre of the vast stage wearing gold crêpe pyjamas scintillating with sequins, and brandished a bugle. Wide gestures of flaunting femininity proclaimed—as she was carried a-top a piano —that a star is a star is a star.'

The show was on. . . .

The curtain went down to rapturous applause and rose again and again. Ginger took six curtain calls. She flung out her arms and told her audience: 'I want your affection and tonight it has been more than I could have expected. You have been a wonderful, gleeful, happy audience.'

Backstage there some 250 telegrams and overseas cables in her suite and at the stage door over another 2,000 were stacked. Crowds of well-wishers clustered round her. Her husband stood quietly aside while Ginger chatted with the press. ('It's been an exhausting time, but it's all been worth it. They were fabulous.') Harold Fielding and Bernard Delfont beamed broadly. Jerry Herman, the American who wrote the songs and music, was also happy: 'I've never been so pleased with a show. Ginger was marvellous.' Herman, responsible for the words and music of *Hello, Dolly!* and *Dear World* apart from *Mame*, had for once sat down to watch one of his shows. Usually, nervously, he prowls. But this time he was confident. With *Mame* in its third year on Broadway he was never in doubt that Ginger would make it a success in London.

Ginger Rogers sipped a ginger ale, though the champagne corks were popping. She flung her arms around the neck of her mother, Lela, who had made her first trip abroad to see her daughter's opening. The woman who over the years had done so much to mould Ginger's successful career was practically in tears of happiness. Ginger quipped: 'I don't care what the critics say. My fabulous mum will give me a good review if nobody else does.' Only the critics themselves who had disappeared to their typewriters were having some uneasy moments.

Next morning the first notices appeared. Few enthused totally about the show itself. Many damned it with the faintest praise. Others, while finding many things in the show that pleased them, also found much to disappoint. One or two were adamantly 'anti'. Some were critical of phases of Ginger's performance, but none was in two minds about the star quality of Ginger and the delight she gave. Ginger had clicked.

B. A. Young (*Financial Times*) said: '*Mame* gave a lot of pleasure to the first-night audience, including me . . . Miss Rogers has only to start dancing to provide the same lift of the heart, the quickening of the breath that she could inspire in her younger days.' Irving Wardle of *The Times* thought 'she glows and radiates a blend of sensual magic and athletic power of a kind I have never seen before in one performer'. Philip Hope-Wallace of the *Guardian* thought her 'adorable in her own well-known screen manner'.

The *Daily Mirror*'s Arthur Thirkell praised her for 'putting most of the kick into the most ballyhooed musical import since *My Fair Lady* . . .'; '. . . astonishingly vivacious', wrote Milton Shulman (*Evening Standard*); Herbert Kretzmer (*Daily Express*) described *Mame* as 'the sort of show that is slowly but inexorably going out of style . . . but it still has a great deal going for it . . . and Ginger Rogers looks stunning, sings with a small but penetrating voice and dances with vigour and a sense of delight'. Felix Barker of the *Evening News* was disappointed in the show because it gave Ginger Rogers little chance of doing the things she does so well but adds 'the lady whom we all love looks peachy'. Peter Lewis (*Daily Mail*) was downbeat about the whole affair but David Nathan of the *Sun* described Ginger as 'a genuine, glittering star . . . it is a one-woman show. Fortunately, they have got the right woman.'

My own view about *Mame* was precisely how I felt when I saw it on Broadway. It has not enough hit songs, breathtaking dancing or sustained humour and it is practically impossible to demand of any star that she should be both attractive and as wacky a character as the offbeat Mame invented by Patrick Dennis. Ginger Rogers is far too wholesome and normal to convince me that she is the authentic curious creation of Dennis. Yet I defy anybody to watch this shining star at Drury Lane without a surge of gaiety and delight which owes nothing to the top-of-the-world feeling he may have vividly experienced when watching her captivate Astaire on the screen in his more vulnerable youth. She warmed me from her first appearance.

As she wisecracked and sang 'Bosom Buddies' with Margaret Courtenay (both tinged with good humoured malice); sentimentalized with 'We Need A Little Christmas' and 'If He Walked Into My Life'; radiated delight with 'That's How Young I Feel'; accepted the affectionate homage of the rest of the cast in the 'Mame' scene; sang 'Open A New Window' with glee and swept on to the stage in clothes that made her look as if her couturier was backed by the Bank of England, one sensed on the first night that even if she sometimes fell short of what one anticipated from the screwball character of Auntie Mame, here was someone who knew what audience-appeal was all about. I found myself thinking that her stand-in, India Adams, possibly had the toughest job in the West End since the girl who deputized for Barbra Streisand in *Funny Girl*.

Harold Fielding read the mixed reviews without a twinge of disappointment or rancour. He said: 'The reviews were exactly what I had expected them to be. The show is a star vehicle for a star lady. It is not in the modern fashion. There is nobody prancing around in the nude. It is a woman's show which will make us a lot of money and give enjoyment to a lot of people.'

He is selling a show-package—a bright evening out—and the super, sparkling ingredient in the package is his star. He can be well content. Thanks to astute showmanship plus the personality and experience of his trump card—Miss Rogers—his gamble was well worth the taking.

Chapter 11

AND WHAT COMES NEXT?

Ginger's fine run of stage success in recent years naturally
raises the question of whether she has decided to abandon films
and filming. I would think not. I cannot believe that such a
long, bright career will be allowed to fizzle out on such a downbeat note as the anti-climax of *Harlow* and a film which, what-
ever its merits or faults, has already been on the shelf for around
five years. I believe that Ginger Rogers is merely biding her
time.

The film business is going through a period of radical change.
The star system, over the past few years, has virtually disappeared. It is an age of big films and small cinemas; creative
people in the film business are running an anxious campaign to
prevent ideas being swamped by audit sheets, shareholders'
meetings, bankers, rapacious agents, the rigid demands of
unions and the often foolishly extravagant demands of the
artists themselves.

It has always been like that in pictures but gradually the
climate seems to be worsening. In the old days studios took
monumental gambles and not all of them came off. But they
failed in a high, wide and handsome way. Now, as Robert
Daniel Graff has said: 'Hollywood is a risk business trying to
act like an insurance agency.'

Ginger, like many of her contemporaries, is disenchanted
with some of the changes. Change there must be, and every
generation creates its own new, up-to-the-minute forms of

expression, but we don't have to accept that *any* change is better than none. The film business was created and built up primarily to entertain. Now the over-permissive, undisciplined and often near-licentious way in which many film-makers work and the direction in which much of the present-day screen fare is drifting make many people impatient, contemptuous and unhappy. I believe that Ginger shares that feeling. Many do.

Deborah Kerr was recently talking illuminatingly and a mite wistfully to Margaret Hinxman, the well-balanced film writer of the *Sunday Telegraph*: 'When I was under contract to MGM, with people like poor Robert Taylor and so many others, the cinema's job was solely entertainment. It filled a public need then. Now the cinema serves so many other purposes; it functions as psychiatrist, politician, message-maker, money-maker and, incidentally, entertainer. But it's no good regretting that things are different. Times have to change.' But reading between the lines, one senses that this eminently intelligent actress does recognize a slide in film standards—or some of them anyway.

Myrna Loy, another of the greats of the days when the cinema was flecked with magic, was equally candid—perhaps more so —when she talked with Rex Reed of the *New York Times*. This elegant comedienne with the retroussé nose and the poised sense of humour has also been acting mainly on the stage for quite a time. She admits that she still likes movies, but she is not in love with the direction in which they're heading. 'I admire some of the people on the screen today, but most of them look like everybody else. In our days we had individuality. Pictures were more sophisticated. All this nudity is too excessive and it is getting very boring. It will be a shame if it upsets people so much that it brings on the need for censorship. I hate censorship. In the cinema there's no mystery. No privacy. And no sex, either. Most of the sex I've seen on the screen looks like an expression of hostility towards sex.'

Ginger Rogers still gets plenty of screen offers and a fair share of screenplays reaches her, but her feelings towards the

modern cinema are quite definite. She insists: 'These days I
think they are making too many tasteless pictures, full of smut
and sex and very little else. Most of today's pictures are just
getting worse.'

Ginger, a moral woman with strong religious feelings, has
gone on record in her official studio biography as saying: 'I have
turned down numerous parts on moral grounds. The women
were unwholesome, dissolute, weak and lawless. All the roles
I have refused have been unnecessarily vulgar. To have to
undress, show how women seduce men, how gutsy you are—
that's for the birds, not for me. I intend never to be a party to
selling the seamy side of life to the young as being normal.
Today they're making happenings, not stories; but there's no
such thing as a happening, there's a reason for everything.'

Fighting, corrosive words they may be, but I believe Ginger
means them wholeheartedly and I think that she will stick to
her belief. She is rich, independent and strong-minded and she
will be prepared to wait for the screenplay that will catch her
imagination and keep to her standards. She is not compelled to
plunge into any dubious mess of words and situations which a
producer, eager to make a quick reputation or a quicker fortune,
dreams up as a 'with-it' film. She has earned the right to pick
and choose—and one cannot blame her for exercising that
prerogative.

But there's no evidence that Ginger Rogers and films have
permanently parted company.

Seventy-three films spread over more than three decades is
an industrious track-record and she, like many of her colleagues
and friends in both Hollywood and Britain in the thirties,
forties and fifties, managed by sheer knowhow to weather some
very indifferent films. Apart from the memorable musicals that
she made with Fred Astaire, not more than a dozen or so of
Ginger's films would be able to stand up to close critical analysis.
Most of the others were simply baubles tossed into the air in the

hope that someone would catch them and perhaps get some brief enjoyment, excitement or relaxation from them. Is that a crime? In these days, when the cinema is perhaps over-emphasised as a major art form, they would either be dismissed by critics with some snide, even contemptuous, witticism or else would be attacked with the ferocity of a heavy ack-ack gun mowing down a butterfly. Yet human beings don't change all that much in a few years. It does not seem to me to be any more reprehensible for a tired professional man to get some passing entertainment from a frothy picture than for him casually to pick up a cheap thriller or 'whodunit' and read himself to sleep.

Nowadays, however, the cinema has tended to become more Significant—with a capital S. Satire is acceptable, but sheer idle frivolity is suspect, sometimes considered shameful. People are constantly probing for messages which they are convinced are trying to escape from under the cap-and-bells. Critics are selective about the comedians on whose professional anatomies they are prepared to sharpen their knives. Buster Keaton, the Marx Brothers, Laurel and Hardy, Harold Lloyd, W. C. Fields, Chaplin, Tati, Larry Semon and Harry Langdon have passed the test and have become cults. One day someone may take time off to make an equally critical, careful and searching analysis of the supremely skilled work done by people like Cary Grant, Jack Lemmon, Myrna Loy, Shirley MacLaine, Walter Matthau, Eve Arden and Carole Lombard; yes, and Ginger Rogers. Few of their films have been designed for posterity; at the very least most of their work has admirably fulfilled a passing need.

In an informative article by Francis Wyndham in the *Sunday Times Magazine* he quoted Ginger thus: 'I'm most grateful to have had that joyous time in motion pictures. It really was a Golden Age of Hollywood. Pictures were talking, they were singing, they were colouring. It was beginning to blossom out: bud and blossom were both present.'

That period is hardly likely to return, just as the millions who would visit the cinema faithfully every week—perhaps twice a week—to dream a dream have shrunk to a comparative few and are unlikely to return in giant numbers in the new age of the cinema. Competition now is too superficial, widespread and fierce.

Ginger survived through over 30 years of filming as one of the indestructibles because she has been the complete professional in an industry which has always demanded a devoted dedication from its workers,—even though it has not always received it and maybe has not fully deserved it. Ben Lyon made a film with Sally Eilers called *Hat Check Girl*. It was so long ago that the *Hell's Angels* star, who later discovered Marilyn Monroe, had to have his memory nudged before he recalled that in *Hat Check Girl* a vivacious newcomer had a small role. It was Ginger Rogers. He remembers an eager youngster who was always alert before the camera 'and', says Ben, 'when she wasn't actually acting she would be watching intently to see what was going on. She was intensely interested in every aspect from the directing to the cameras and even the work of the gaffers (technicians).'

Later, Ben and his wife Bebe Daniels, who was a star of *Forty Second Street*, in which Ginger also made an effective appearance, came to know her fairly well, for in those early days Hollywood was a far more tightly knit community than now. 'She had to succeed partly because of her complete dedication,' Ben told me. 'Never late on the set and never temperamental. She knew her lines and was responsive to direction. Yes, a real pro,' said Ben. It was a pro talking and he could not have given the girl a greater reference.

When, at times, Ginger later found herself contractually trapped and put to work in some poorish picture she never 'coasted'. She always played the part as if it might be the one that could win an Oscar and this was not lost on the powerful magnates who ran Hollywood—the moguls like Sam Goldwyn, Harry Cohn, Jack Warner, David Selznick, Louis B. Mayer and Darryl Zanuck.

And what comes next?

In comedy, her real forte, she had gaiety and sparkle which lit up the screen. She could be sunny, or she could toss off a well-timed, crisp wisecrack with a caustic tinge which made it sound wittier than the writer may even have visualized. This latter gift sparked in such films as *Roxie Hart* and *Stage Door*. In films like *Storm Warning*, *Black Widow* and *Tight Spot* she showed a tougher streak. *Tom, Dick and Harry*, *Bachelor Mother* and *The Major And The Minor* were typical of the amiable comedies to which she brought a brand of lighthearted warmth that tickled the audience like a glass of bubbly.

Looking back on the past few sentences I note that I have written in the past tense; but this is no film obituary. Despite all the glamour and enticement of the theatre Ginger will be back in the cinema. The era to which she contributed much and which began to change a few years ago is perhaps past for ever. Films and filming will never be quite the same either in technique or even in content. I doubt though that Ginger will differ much.

If she had done nothing else she would be remembered for her share in the niche that she and Fred Astaire built for themselves, just as Nelson Eddy and Jeanette Macdonald did, and Mickey Rooney and Judy Garland in the *Andy Hardy* series; as Myrna Loy did with William Powell in the *Thin Man* comedies and, for a brief time, Garbo with John Gilbert.

There could be no doubt what the Astaire-Rogers musicals represented. Freud would have had difficulty in finding anything but sheer, airy escapism in the titles of the films alone. They amply fulfilled their job of wafting people into a world where logic bowed low to romance and the kitchen sink was hidden behind gossamer drapes.

During the ten-year span between *The Story of Vernon And Irene Castle* and *The Barkleys Of Broadway* she was repeatedly asked why she hadn't made another film with Fred. 'Because nobody's ever asked us,' she would reply tactfully and truthfully. It was wise to end the association when they did, for though the standard of the films never perceptibly flagged the box-office receipts began to inch down and in the cinema world you are only as good as your last grosses.

The musicals, starting after oil was unexpectedly struck with their sudden success as a pair of featured players in *Flying Down To Rio*, were built on a regular formula. The stories were slim and inconsequential, usually centring around minor romantic complications with Fred falling for the girl, diffidently wooing her and finally getting her, Ginger offering merely token resistance. Above all, they had to be clean, gay and easy on both the eye and the ear.

The last was most important so nobody but the top light-music tunesmiths of the day—such as Gershwin, Berlin and Kern—was hired to write the songs. As a result the series produced some of the greatest, most evergreen ditties of their *genre*. They have been played and recorded endlessly by every type of musical combination from symphony orchestras to tavern piano-thumpers, via Palm Court trios. They have been sung by vocalists great and humble. Above all, they have been bawled tunelessly and nostalgically in millions of bathrooms, but they have never lost their lilt, romance or cheeky wit. Somewhere, in some place, every minute of every day, a melody from one of the Gershwin, Cole Porter, Berlin clan is being played or sung.

There had to be several striking dance situations—an opportunity for Fred to go inimitably solo and often a similar chance for Ginger—and two or three song and/or dance duets for the famous team. And, trump up the sleeve, there had to be a dazzling finale, with the two leading into a striking ensemble with a splash of extras and bit players and a whirling, swirling, carefree, frenetic fade-out that would send the customers home in a mood to dance down the High Street. It proved to be not a bad formula.

The films also demanded that Fred and Ginger should be supported by first class acting talent. There were variations in personnel, of course, but gradually there was built up what was virtually a top-cast repertory company. The two most regular males were Eric Blore and Erik Rhodes. Blore was a British actor who went to Hollywood around the same time that Ginger arrived. With his pouting, tremulous lower lip, sly smile, knowing eyes, bland, unctuous voice and dignified, perambulating walk he became the perennial butler, valet or head waiter, always at hand with a soothing word or a wily, insulting barb.

Rhodes, an American stage actor, was the sleek, sometimes suave, sometimes excitable Continental, available as gigolo, hotel manager, co-respondent, restaurateur or con-man. Edward Everett Horton, curiously, played in only three of the series yet somehow seemed an integral part of the company. Always teetering nervously on the edge of a nervous breakdown, permanently harassed, he was invaluable as the hapless husband, the business-man, the lawyer, the bemused friend of the hero, the fall guy.

One question constantly arose concerning Nelson Eddy and Jeanette Macdonald: were they ever married? The answer, of course, was 'No', as Jeanette's long-suffering husband, Gene Raymond, good-humouredly pointed out incessantly. The same question often arose concerning Ginger and Fred. Again the answer is 'No'. But an even more persistent question when they are discussed (which is often) is whether Ginger was just the 'junior partner' in the team and whether she was 'carried' by the brilliance of Astaire's hoofing.

Only one person I can think of has ever questioned Ginger's skill as a dancer. That is Chita Rivera, a pert, lissom young actress who is herself no mean dancer, as she proved when winning an Oscar for *West Side Story*. Chita is reported by William Hall of the *Evening News* as saying: 'There aren't many dancers around today, not good ones. Gwen Verdon, Juliet Prowse, they're good. Rita Hayworth had great style. But Ginger Rogers wasn't a good dancer. Not by our standards. There's a difference between being a dedicated dancer and a star who is dancing. Astaire did the dancing, if you watch those movies closely.' Since I can scarcely do a Sir Roger de Coverley without falling on my abashed face I cannot argue, except to say that I think Miss Rivera is talking out of the back of her attractive little head.

Edward Everett Horton told me when he was visiting London on holiday: 'Of course Fred created, with Hermes Pan, most of the dances in those films; of course he led the ceremonies. Isn't that the man's job in dancing? But, believe me, Ginger was great. She contributed her full fifty per cent in making them such a great team. She could follow Fred as if one brain was thinking. She blended with his every step and mood immaculately. He was able to do dances on the screen that would have been impossible to risk if he hadn't had a partner like Ginger—as skilful as she was attractive.'

When the two eventually split and Ginger moved off to concentrate on straight acting, Fred continued with his screen dancing, and was partnered by some of the most alluring girls in the business. The first girl he had danced with on the screen was Joan Crawford. Later, when he 'lost' Ginger, he found an array of fresh partners. He teamed with such dancing lovelies as Eleanor Powell ('Too individualistic for Fred,' insisted Buddy Bradley), Paulette Goddard, Marjorie Reynolds, Rita Hayworth, Joan Leslie, Lucille Bremner, Joan Caulfield, Olga San Juan, Judy Garland, Ann Miller, Betty Hutton and Barrie Chase.

But he never found another dancing partner like Ginger, the girl who added zest to Fred's legs and punctuated the poetry of his educated feet. They were the perfectly blended gin-and-It.

What does Fred think about it? In 1966, the New York Gallery of Modern Art paid tribute to Ginger in the form of a short festival of her films. The gallery's film curator, Raymond Rohauer, interviewed Ginger and mentioned that he had met Fred Astaire at the San Francisco Film Festival a couple of months before. Rohauer quoted Fred as saying: 'Ginger was brilliantly effective. She made everything work for her. Actually she made things very fine for both of us and she deserves most of the credit for our success.'

Ginger has always admitted freely that she enjoyed working with Fred. She respected him as a super craftsman, helpful and unselfish. 'We never had quarrels. Of course, we had strong arguments and differences of opinion—that's common with any artistic marriage. But we never had harsh words. Once we differed bitterly over a matter, but even then we didn't have a slanging match; we just didn't speak till we had cooled off!' That is a fairly remarkable record considering the hours they were flung together in a strained atmosphere when going through the inevitable slog of preparing for a new film. Often it meant an eighteen-hour day and Ginger has admitted that sometimes her feet were bleeding and she was so tired that she could barely eat or drag herself to bed for a few hours.

For Ginger, Fred, Hermes Pan and all concerned with the productions were perfectionists. They had set themselves such a high standard that they could not afford to relax their efforts. On the whole, it is amazing that the two could share such a long professional association without one or the other blowing their tops irretrievably.

It explains why they barely mixed with each other socially except when they happened to meet at mutual friends' houses. It was certainly not because they did not get along, as one or two columnists at first tried to insinuate but quickly gave up the fruitless task. According to an interview in New York's *Morning Telegraph* Ginger insists that gossip of a feud with Fred Astaire was 'just a lot of studio hoopla. Fred and I don't see each other very often, but in some ways we will always have a firm friendship.' Though her all-time favourite leading man was Cary Grant, she says in the same interview, Astaire was her 'favourite dancing partner'.

Ever since they had first met in New York they had had a

warm regard for each other. In Francis Wyndham's story about Ginger in the *Sunday Times Magazine* he quotes her as saying: 'I loved Fred so, and I mean that in the nicest, warmest way: I had such affection for him artistically. I think that experience with Fred was a divine blessing. It blessed me, I know, and I don't think blessings are one-sided.'

There are probably some who think that to invoke the word 'blessing' in connection with such a temporal matter as a Hollywood screen twosome was an overreach. The RKO studio chiefs and their stockholders, revelling in the popularity of the dancing favourites, would have regarded it as something of an understatement.

It was not only at the RKO studio that Ginger was a welcome employee. During the course of her long screen career she has worked for virtually every major studio in the business, except that of Walt Disney.

Perhaps, on reflection, that is the answer to Ginger's script problem? Nobody, as far as I am aware, has ever knocked the Disney organization for creating unseemly feminine characters, except for an odd witch or two in its cartoons.

Chapter 12

WHAT MAKES GINGER TICK?

Leonard Louis Levinson, a humorous, amiable, shaggy bear of an American, has produced a couple of books called *Webster's Unafraid Dictionary* consisting of daffy definitions, parodies, wisecracks, epigrams and witticisms—some original, some borrowed—on a variety of subjects.

Hollywood is not neglected. Some of the entries are merely slick, amusing gags; others have more than a ring of truth. A man named Tom Jenk, for instance, is credited with the description of Hollywood as 'a locality where people without reputation try to live up to it'. It is true enough that many people with a minimal talent either for acting or for living perpetually claw for a place in the sun. Sunset Boulevard is cluttered with such scrambled egos.

Yet there are others—and Ginger Rogers is one of them—who have managed to live a successful and contented lifetime in 'the most beautiful jail in the world'. To do it you need strong principles and a sane capacity for keeping your feet on the ground. Once you begin to believe your own publicity and start to 'go Hollywood' you are a lost soul.

Ginger's own particular strength for survival in this rarefied atmosphere is based on good health, a generous sense of humour and strong religious convictions. She was brought up believing in Christian Science and she has never wavered in her beliefs. Only once has she been seriously ill, when she contracted pneumonia in Manhattan. She says: 'I met that problem, as I meet all my problems, great and small, with prayer. But in such a situation you need help. So I called on a Christian Science practitioner—not a doctor. I was helped and, through God's goodness, I was healed.'

She calls on God's help a great deal and, without a shred of self-consciousness, His name crops up considerably in her everyday conversation. 'As a Christian Scientist, I am convinced that a spiritual investment is far more gratifying in the long run than a financial one. You have got to have a belief in something that is going to pay you spiritual dividends.' She is a regular churchgoer, at one time attending the La Brea and Hollywood Boulevard Church. Now she and her husband worship at the Twenty-Eighth Church of Christ Scientist in the fashionable Westwood neighbourhood.

Through her mother's influence she came quite spontaneously as a child towards her faith. It was not a conscious process and the first steps were uncomplicated; but it taught her an innate sense of right and wrong and the belief that religion never fails you, though you can easily fail it.

So, in the brittle atmosphere of Hollywood where some of the most talented and delightful people I have met brush shoulders with characters I would not even introduce to a self-respecting viper, Ginger has kept her nose clean throughout. I wrote to a playwright-journalist friend of mine in New York, Tedwell Chapman, and asked him to dig among the magazine files for any information that would help me to evaluate this pleasant woman and actress. He replied: 'I know you are *not* looking for dirt and scandal. It's a good thing, for if there *is* any then the papers seem to have missed out on it.'

As an attractive and successful actress it was to be expected that her name would be linked with those of many eligible men, for the average Hollywood journalist is not usually averse to putting two and two together and making six. But apart from the men she married her name seems to have been linked with only two. In the early days director Mervyn Le Roy was a regular 'date'; later she was seen around a great deal with Greg Bautzer, the handsome, eligible lawyer. But which actress has not, at some time, been linked with Bautzer? Tall, elegant, witty and richly successful, Greg Bautzer, who was later to marry the young British actress Dana Wynter, was the dream escort for the unattached girl, with connections with the best people and an entrée to the most glamorous functions in Hollywood.

The fact that Ginger has been married five times has naturally caused many tongues to wag. She regards her marriages as her private concern, talks little about them and certainly not more than superficially. What emerges is that despite four broken marriages she does not treat marriage lightly; it is highly important to her.

Over ten years ago, in London, she said firmly: 'Marriage I love, divorce I hate.' Though she does not discuss it freely she has clearly given a lot of thought to her failure in the marriage stakes, for she admits that failure hurts her. On her previous London visit she remarked, with astounding candour, that 'I am young—almost a child—at heart. I'm adolescent, immature, with so much to learn. That, I think, is why I have been so unlucky in my emotional life. I pick the wrong sort of guy and, after all, love and hate are the sort of things that you can't do very much about. I don't think age difference matters when you are aglow with love.'

Her first marriage was virtually an adolescent boy-meets-girl affair; her second was at a time when her career was riding high and that of her husband was not progressing; her third could be put down to a wartime romance; her fourth was the outcome of a romantic courtship in romantic Riviera surroundings.

Now, in maturity, she seems to have found the married happiness that has always been so elusive. She and William Marshall had known each other for some 20 years—they met on the set of *Kitty Foyle*—before they married a few years ago.

Both were secure in their careers and both of those careers have flourished. Says Ginger: 'The most important quality in a husband is a quality of mind. It covers many things. If he has that you can find a platform to stand on.'

Bill Marshall certainly has that quality of mind. He shares his wife's belief in religion; her liking for artistic things; her passion for outdoor living; and, through all the ballyhoo of her stardom, he has shared her reticence to lay their marriage out in the open and invite dissection. Bill merely says: 'I have known Ginger for about 30 years and she has never changed. Her beauty comes from within. She is a good, sane woman who is civil and simple, loving and considerate.' After that testimonial there does not seem very much that needs saying.

One of the advantages of their marriage is that there is no chance of that awkward, embarrassing possibility of his being referred to as 'Mr. Ginger Rogers'. Marshall is a success in his own right. He has a financial interest in *Mame*, but that represents only one of his reasons for being in London. He is busily negotiating the release in Britain of his film *The Confession*. He is also busy with the coming publication of his novel *The Deal* which is based on his knowledge of Hollywood and is said to be a really forthright picture of that strange little world. He has also been busy finishing another book.

A one-time singer with Fred Waring's orchestra, he is now a producer, writer and director. He is also wealthy—maybe not so rich as his very rich actress wife, but still gratifyingly well off, with two ranches and a plantation in Jamaica. Ginger admits that she is extremely rich and has always proved herself an astute negotiator over a dollar. 'I have a healthy respect for what money can buy in this material world,' she insists. 'But money is by no means my god. Money is not the root of all evil but the *love* of it is.'

Marshall is a crack shot and a low-handicap golfer—both keen interests of Ginger's—and neither is a social gadabout. So the two seem admirably attuned to each other. Perhaps it is proof that Ginger has grown gracefully into maturity. In the *Morning Telegraph* she is reported as saying: 'I'm darned proud that I've finally grown up. If someone came up to me and said "Okay, Ginger, you've had it—there's nothing else for you to do", well I'd say "Fine" and I would go home and paint and I would be happy.'

The fact that Ginger has never been blessed with children has always been a regret to her, and Ginger and her husband are planning to adopt a child. It was a joint idea and whichever child is lucky enough to be picked can be sure of plenty of loving, plenty of travel and the best education that money can buy.

The question of age is another subject about which Ginger is reluctant to talk overmuch. She has always thought that age is unimportant. 'There's too much emphasis on age, whether young, old or middle,' thinks Ginger. 'Youth is in the mind, not in the condition of your flesh.' Not that she is stuffy about references to her age; after all, the evidence is merely in the reference books and not in Ginger's eyes, smile and trim figure—5 feet 5 inches and an 'acting' weight of eight stone.

During her London season of *Mame* she was guest of honour at one of the lunches of the Variety Club of Great Britain, the lavishly generous charity organization for under-privileged children. She was the first to laugh when actor Kenneth More, proposing a toast, read from her biography 'She was born in the Year of our Lord' and stopped at the last word. In her reply Ginger grinned widely as she said that she was willing to sell herself as an antique to the highest bidder to raise funds for Variety.

Over the years she has built herself a sound philosophy. She is interested in her old films (unlike Fred Astaire, who can scarcely bear to watch them) though she does not dwell on them. But her concern is always for the project on which she is working. 'You can't walk through *Mame*,' she explains. 'It is fun, but it is strenuous. I find that water's running off my back every night.' She has come far from the days when she would worry and try to keep up with the Joneses. She has said: 'Now they can give it all to three Joan Crawfords and seven Bette Davises and, believe me, I wouldn't care.'

Ginger, non-smoker, non-drinker (though irrevocably hooked on every combination of ice-cream), has never lost her passion for sport and games. She swims regularly, plays golf, fishes, shoots and plays tennis. When she was a young star in *Girl Crazy* she would play on the public courts between rehearsals and shows. Later she graduated to tougher tennis, though she was never a champion. But in her court at her Hollywood home she can still hold her own with the professionals. She is a charter member of the West Side tennis club in California and won a Pimm's Cup Award in the mixed doubles finals at a tournament at Palm Springs. She once even appeared—and acquitted herself well—on the centre court at Forest Hills during the international championships. 'I did not make much progress,' smiles Ginger. 'I put that down to two things. I wasn't nearly good enough and I had to dress appropriately for the occasion. I am better at tennis when I can just wear a shirt, short pants and sneakers.' She has even won a gold medal at table tennis in the Los Angeles tournament.

It is this array of interests—she is a Daughter of the American Revolution (one of her mother's ancestors having fought at Bunker's Hill), a member of Jackson County Sheriff's Posse at Oregon and an honorary admiral in the Texas Navy—which helps to retain the enthusiasm and pep that have sustained her through those countless films and onerous stage shows. That and a strict attention to diet.

Ginger claims that she is not a health food faddist. 'I'm a meat and potatoes girl,' she insists. 'But I do insist on as many vegetables and fruits that are in season as I can get, and I don't drink coffee. I think too much caffeine's bad—and anyway I don't need stimulants. In fact, my golden rule,' she told Joan

What makes Ginger tick?

Reeder, 'is to remember Bill's slogan of "E.H."—which simply means "Eat Half".'

Away from sport, her main interests are painting, sculpting and music. Mary Holland of the *Observer* was impressed with her 'vividly attractive, technically competent work.' Miss Holland also noticed, on a visit to Ginger's home, an oil painting of Katharine Cornell's New York house overlooking the Hudson River in winter. It was unfinished. Ginger remarked: 'It's gone cold on me and when a painting goes cold it stays cold.' Fortunately, few things go cold on Ginger.

Music is an absorbing interest of Ginger's. When Roy Plomley introduced her on his *Desert Island Discs* programme on the BBC he found her 'splendid to work with and wonderfully co-operative. The programme's never been less complicated. Her musical tastes were obviously catholic, though they leaned towards classical music.' Eventually, her selections included 'Salut d'Amour', which she used to sing as a small girl, Tchaikowsky's *Romeo and Juliet, Rhapsody in C Major* by Dohnanyi, played by her old friend Eileen Joyce, *Symphonie Espagnole* played by Yehudi Menuhin ('He's played this for me alone more times than he knows'), 'Tangerine' played by Harry James ('I love the Big Band sound'), MacHenry Boatwright singing 'He's Got The Whole World In His Hands', a wonderful spiritual, and for auld lang syne Fred Astaire and herself singing 'My One And Only Highland Fling'—the one disc the pair made together because of contractual problems. Plomley asked her how she would fare on a desert island. 'I could look after myself,' she said. 'I wouldn't try to escape if I had these records, my painting canvases and equipment and Mary Baker Eddy's book *Science and Health*.'

Ginger sums up her feelings about life by saying: 'In everything that I do I learn and try to put it to use. I have learned to go through life not into it. It's like a boat. You mustn't let the water in or you're sunk. Of course, I've made mistakes and I have had failures, but I do not dwell on them because people don't care about garbage. When I make a mistake it's like a bad leaf on a lettuce—I throw it out into the waste basket.'

Of her career she says: 'I'm just an image that goes round the world and what I try to give is a little joy, laughter, glee and romance. That's an actress's privilege. It's not ego but gratitude when I find that people remember me and want my autograph. It is probably their way of thanking me for the entertainment I have always tried to give them.'

It is no bad idea to seek the opinions of those with whom a person works.

Harold Fielding paid her the greatest compliment when she went off for a deserved two weeks' holiday. He replaced her with another big name—Juliet Prowse—and spent another £15,000 on a special wardrobe for Miss Prowse. He said: 'Only by replacing Ginger with an artist as fine and glamorous as Juliet and by giving the audience a bonus in the shape of a lavish new wardrobe could we fairly compensate them for missing Ginger Rogers in *Mame*.'

Roger Clifford, his press agent, was as enthusiastic, remarking that 'she's wonderful. No trouble at all.' That, as newspapermen know, is a great accolade from a publicity man, usually aged before his time by star temperament.

I spoke to a couple of the cast. Margaret Courtenay, playing her first musical and enjoying it with zest, said of Ginger: 'She is quite super on the stage and there's absolutely no great starry stuff about her. At rehearsals she mixed with the kids and they adore her.

'She is, though, a very private person and I barely see her except on the stage. She has to get to the theatre long before the rest of us and leaves much later, so there's little I can say about her as a person except that it's great knowing her.'

The fact that Ginger is a dedicated professional was swiftly confirmed by Barry Kent, who plays her husband in the show. Barry told me that when he got the job he could not help remembering his boyhood in Southsea. 'That was when I fell in love with Ginger Rogers,' he told me. 'I was in my very young salad days and I used to go and revel in her films, thought how wonderful she was and envied Fred Astaire. I would have thought people were mad if they had prophesied that one day I would be playing opposite her at Drury Lane. I didn't know quite what to expect when we first started rehearsing. After all, it was the first time I'd played opposite such a legendary star.

'But at first rehearsal she put me and the others at our ease so pleasantly. I guess, maybe, that's why she has stayed at the top.' Kent also remembers that when he had an accident on stage, hitting his head on an iron pillar, he had to miss three shows. He recalls that Ginger took the trouble to ring Barry's wife and chat with her a long while, sympathizing.

It's fragmentary remarks such as these that add up to a remark made by one of the backstage staff. 'She's a great gal—a real toff,' he confided to me.

'Nobody's ever called me a beauty,' Ginger has said. Perhaps she missed what *Vogue* said of her once: 'Her face is tanned and healthy. Her smile is wholesome and roguish. Her figure is perfect. It is a lesson to us all. From the back she might be a very young girl.'

It was Garson Kanin, writing of Ginger Rogers, who summarized it all by saying: 'A movie star is a creation the substance of which, like a painting or a statue or a symphony, does not age. People grow older but stars remain.'

This is a star whom we would be enchanted to retain in London for ever.

POSTSCRIPT

Just as there is always someone in a party who has not heard a joke—however much of a chestnut—so there is always someone ignorant of the most common legend.

Such as how did Ginger Rogers acquire her widely known name?

For you, young sir and young miss, this is how Virginia McMath became Ginger Rogers, and I hope it will relieve those older readers who must be thinking by now that I had forgotten to include this piece of intelligence.

The 'Rogers' was the surname of her well-loved stepfather who legally adopted her. The 'Ginger'? Well, it seems that her cousin, Phyllis Fraser, who was to become her closest friend, found it difficult to get her childish tongue around the name 'Virginia'. It constantly came out sounding like 'Gingah'.

So be it.

Phyllis Fraser is now the wife of that prosperous, prolific American publisher and joke collector, Bennett Cerf. And, as in all the best fairy stories, they are living happily ever after.

APPENDIX

THE FILMS OF GINGER ROGERS

1930

Young Man Of Manhattan, with Claudette Colbert, Charles Ruggles, Norman Foster. Director: Monta Bell (Paramount)

Queen High, with Charles Ruggles, Frank Morgan, Betty Garde. Director: Fred Newmeyer (Paramount)

The Sap From Syracuse, with Jack Oakie, Verree Teasdale. Director: Ed Sutherland (Paramount)

Follow The Leader, with Ed Wynn, Ethel Merman, Preston Foster. Director: Norman Taurog (Paramount)

1931

Honour Among Lovers, with Claudette Colbert, Fredric March, Pat O'Brien, Ralph Morgan, Charles Ruggles. Director: Dorothy Arzner (Paramount)

The Tip Off, with Robert Armstrong, Eddie Quillan. Director: Albert Rogell (Pathé)

Suicide Fleet, with Robert Armstrong, William Boyd, James Gleason. Director: Albert Rogell (Pathé)

1932

Carnival Boat, with William Boyd, Hobart Bosworth, Edgar Kennedy, Marie Prevost. Director: Albert Rogell (Pathé)

The Tenderfoot, with Joe E. Brown, Lew Cody, Vivien Oakland, Ralph Ince. Director: Ray Enright (First National)

The Thirteenth Guest, with Lyle Talbot, J. Farrell McDonald, Paul Hurst. Director: Albert Ray (Monogram)

Appendix

Hat Check Girl, with Ben Lyon, Sally Eilers, Monroe Owsley, Noel Madison. Director: Sidney Lanfield (Fox)

You Said A Mouthful, with Joe E. Brown, Guinn Williams, Preston Foster. Director: Lloyd Bacon (First National)

1933

Forty Second Street, with Warner Baxter, Bebe Daniels, George Brent, Ruby Keeler, Dick Powell, Una Merkel, Guy Kibbee. Director: Lloyd Bacon (Warners)

Broadway Bad, with Joan Blondell, Ricardo Cortez, Victor Jory, Adrienne Ames, Donald Crisp. Director: Sidney Lanfield (Fox)

Gold Diggers of 1933, with Warren William, Joan Blondell, Aline MacMahon, Ruby Keeler, Dick Powell, Ned Sparks, Guy Kibbee. Director: Mervyn Le Roy (Warners)

Professional Sweetheart, with Gregory Ratoff, Franklyn Pangborn, Zasu Pitts, Frank McHugh, Allen Jenkins, Edgar Kennedy, Norman Foster. Director: William Seiter (RKO)

A Shriek In The Night, with Lyle Talbot, Arthur Hoyt, Louise Beavers, Purnell Pratt. Director: Albert Ray (Allied)

Don't Bet On Love, with Lew Ayres, Charles Grapewin, Shirley Grey. Director: Murray Roth (Universal)

Sitting Pretty, with Jack Oakie, Thelma Todd, Jack Haley, Gregory Ratoff, Lew Cody, Harry Revel. Director: Harry Joe Brown (Paramount)

Chance At Heaven, with Joel McCrea, Andy Devine, Lucien Littlefield, George Meeker, Marian Nixon, Ann Shoemaker. Director: William Seiter (RKO)

Flying Down To Rio, with Gene Raymond, Dolores Del Rio, Franklyn Pangborn, Fred Astaire, Eric Blore. Director: Thornton Freeland (RKO)

1934

Rafter Romance, with Norman Foster, Laura Hope Crews, Robert Benchley, Guinn Williams. Director: William Seiter (RKO)

Appendix

Finishing School, with Billie Burke, Frances Dee, Bruce Cabot, Beulah Bondi, John Halliday. Directors: Wandah Tuchock and George Nicols Jr. (RKO)

Twenty Million Sweethearts, with Dick Powell, Allen Jenkins, Pat O'Brien, Grant Mitchell, Joseph Cawthorne. Director: Ray Enright (First National)

Change Of Heart, with Janet Gaynor, Charles Farrell, James Dunn, Jane Darwell, Shirley Temple. Director: John G. Blystone (Fox)

Upper World, with Warren William, Mary Astor, Dickie Moore, J. Carroll Naish, Andy Devine. Director: Roy Del Ruth (Warners)

The Gay Divorcee (British title: *The Gay Divorce*), with Fred Astaire, Alice Brady, Edward Everett Horton, Erik Rhodes, Eric Blore, Betty Grable. Director: Mark Sandrich (RKO)

Romance In Manhattan, with Francis Lederer, J. Farrell Mac-Donald, Donald Meek. Director: Stephen Roberts (RKO)

1935

Roberta, with Fred Astaire, Irene Dunne, Randolph Scott, Helen Westley, Claire Dodd, Victor Marconi, Lucille Ball. Director: William Seiter (RKO)

Star Of Midnight, with William Powell, Paul Kelly, Gene Lockhart, Ralph Morgan, Leslie Fenton. Director: Stephen Roberts (RKO)

Top Hat, with Fred Astaire, Edward Everett Horton, Erik Rhodes, Eric Blore, Lucille Ball, Helen Broderick. Director: Mark Sandrich (RKO)

In Person, with George Brent, Alan Mowbray, Edgar Kennedy, Grant Mitchell. Director: William Seiter (RKO)

1936

Follow The Fleet, with Fred Astaire, Randolph Scott, Tony Martin, Harriet Hilliard, Betty Grable, Lucille Ball. Director, Mark Sandrich (RKO)

Appendix

Swing Time, with Fred Astaire, Helen Broderick, Victor Moore, Betty Furness, Eric Blore. Director: George Stevens (RKO)

1937

Shall We Dance?, with Fred Astaire, Edward Everett Horton, Jerome Cowan, Harriet Hoctor, Ann Shoemaker, Eric Blore. Director: Nathaniel Shilkret (RKO)

Stage Door, with Katharine Hepburn, Constance Collier, Adolphe Menjou, Lucille Ball, Gail Patrick, Andrea Leeds, Ann Miller, Jack Carson, Eve Arden, Ralph Forbes, Franklyn Pangborn. Director: Gregory La Cava (RKO)

1938

Having Wonderful Time, with Douglas Fairbanks Jr., Red Skelton, Lucille Ball, Eve Arden, Lee Bowman, Jack Carson, Donald Meek. Director: Alfred Santell (RKO)

Vivacious Lady, with James Stewart, Charles Coburn, Beulah Bondi, Franklyn Pangborn, Jack Carson, Hattie McDaniel. Director: George Stevens (RKO)

Carefree, with Fred Astaire, Ralph Bellamy, Franklyn Pangborn Jack Carson. Director: Mark Sandrich (RKO)

1939

The Story Of Vernon And Irene Castle, with Fred Astaire, Edna May Oliver, Walter Brennan, Janet Beecher, Clarence Derwent. Director: H. C. Potter (RKO)

Bachelor Mother, with David Niven, Charles Coburn, Ernest Truex, Frank Albertson. Director: Garson Kanin (RKO)

Fifth Avenue Girl, with Verree Teasdale, Walter Connolly, Tim Holt, Louis Calhern, Franklyn Pangborn, Jack Carson. Director: Gregory La Cava (RKO)

1940

Primrose Path, with Joel McCrea, Marjorie Rambeau, Henry Travers, Miles Mander. Director: Gregory La Cava (RKO)

Appendix

Lucky Partners, with Ronald Colman, Jack Carson, Spring Byington, Harry Davenport. Director: Lewis Milestone (RKO)

Kitty Foyle, with Dennis Morgan, Gladys Cooper, Ernest Cossart, Eduardo Ciannelli. Director: Sam Wood (RKO)

1941

Tom, Dick And Harry, with George Murphy, Burgess Meredith, Phil Silvers, Alan Marshall. Director: Garson Kanin (RKO)

1942

Roxie Hart, with George Montgomery, Adolphe Menjou, Nigel Bruce, Lynne Overman, Sara Allgood, Phil Silvers, Spring Byington, Helen Reynolds, William Frawley. Director: William A. Wellman (20th Century-Fox)

Tales Of Manhattan, with Henry Fonda, Roland Young, Gail Patrick, Cesar Romero. Director: Julien Duvivier (20th Century-Fox)

The Major And The Minor, with Ray Milland, Robert Benchley, Rita Johnson, Diana Lynn. Director: Billy Wilder (Paramount)

Once Upon A Honeymoon, with Cary Grant, Albert Dekker, Walter Slezak, Albert Basserman. Director: Leo McCarey (RKO)

1943

Tender Comrade, with Robert Ryan, Ruth Hussey, Patricia Collinge, Mady Christians, Jane Darwell, Kim Hunter. Director: Edward Dmytryk (RKO)

1944

Lady in The Dark, with Ray Milland, Jon Hall, Barry Sullivan, Warner Baxter, Mischa Auer, Billy Daniels, Gail Russell. Director: Mitchell Leisen (Paramount)

Appendix

I'll Be Seeing You, with Joseph Cotten, Shirley Temple, Tom Tully, Spring Byington, Chill Wills. Director: William Dieterle (Selznick-United Artists)

1945

Weekend At The Waldorf, with Walter Pidgeon, Van Johnson, Lana Turner, Keenan Wynn, Edward Arnold, Phyllis Thaxter, Robert Benchley, Leon Ames, Irving Bacon, George Zucco. Director: Robert Z. Leonard (MGM)

1946

Heartbeat, with Jean Pierre Aumont, Adolphe Menjou, Melville Cooper, Basil Rathbone, Eduardo Ciannelli, Henry Stephenson. Director: Sam Wood (RKO)

Magnificent Doll, with David Niven, Peggy Wood, Burgess Meredith, Horace McNally. Director: Frank Borzage (Universal)

1947

It Had To Be You, with Cornel Wilde, Ron Randell, Spring Byington. Directors: Don Hartman and Rudolph Maté (Columbia)

1949

The Barkleys Of Broadway, with Fred Astaire, Billie Burke, Oscar Levant, Gale Robbins, George Zucco. Director: Charles Walters (MGM)

Perfect Strangers (British title: *Too Dangerous To Love*) with Dennis Morgan, Thelma Ritter, Margalo Gilmore, Paul Ford. Director: Bretaigne Windust (Warners)

Storm Warning, with Doris Day, Ronald Reagan, Steve Cochran. Director: Stuart Heisler (Warners)

1951

The Groom Wore Spurs, with John Litel, Jack Carson, Joan Davis. Director: Richard Whorf (Universal)

Appendix

1952

We're Not Married, with David Wayne, Victor Moore, Marilyn Monroe, Paul Douglas, Eve Arden, Mitzi Gaynor, Jane Darwell, Eddie Bracken, Louis Calhern, Zsa Zsa Gabor, Fred Allen. Director: Edmund Goulding (20th Century-Fox)

Monkey Business, with Cary Grant, Marilyn Monroe, Hugh Marlowe, Charles Coburn. Director: Howard Hawks (20th Century-Fox)

Dreamboat, with Clifton Webb, Jeff Hunter, Fred Clark, Anne Francis, Elsa Lanchester, Ray Collins. Director: Claude Binyon (20th Century-Fox)

1953

Forever Female, with William Holden, Paul Douglas, James Gleason, Marjorie Rambeau, Patricia Crowley. Director: Irving Rapper (Paramount)

1954

Black Widow, with Van Heflin, George Raft, Gene Tierney, Otto Kruger, Reginald Gardiner, Peggy Ann Garner. Director: Nunnally Johnson (20th Century-Fox)

Beautiful Stranger (American title: *Twist Of Fate*), with Stanley Baker, Herbert Lom, Jacques Bergerac, Margaret Rawlings, Eddie Byrne. Director: David Miller (British Lion)

1955

Tight Spot, with Edward G. Robinson, Brian Keith, Lucy Marlowe, Lorne Greene. Director: Phil Karlson (Columbia)

1956

The First Travelling Saleslady, with Barry Nelson, Carol Channing, Clint Eastwood, David Brian, James Arness. Director: Arthur Lubin (RKO)

Teenage Rebel, with Michael Rennie, Louise Beavers, Irene Hervey, Warren Berlinger, Mildred Natwick, Betty Lou Keim. Director: Edmund Goulding (20th Century-Fox)

Appendix

1957

Oh Men! Oh Women!, with David Niven, Barbara Rush, Tony Randall, Dan Dailey. Director: Nunnally Johnson (20th Century-Fox)

1964

The Confession, with Ray Milland, Cecil Kellaway, Barbara Eden, Carl Schell, Michael Azzara. Director: William Dieterle (William Marshall Productions)

1965

Harlow, with Carol Lynley, Efrem Zimbalist, Hurd Hatfield, Hermione Baddeley, Barry Sullivan, Audrey Totter. Director: Alex Segal (Magna Pictures Corporation)

INDEX

Index

Index

Index

Index

Index

Index

Index

Index

Index